Delivered
A death-defying journey into heaven and hell

By Tamara Laroux

Copyright © 2010 by Tamara Laroux

Delivered
A death-defying journey into heaven and hell
by Tamara Laroux

Printed in the United States of America

ISBN 9781597819503

All rights reserved solely by the author. The author guarantees all contents are original and do not infringe upon the legal rights of any other person or work. No part of this book may be reproduced in any form without the permission of the author. The views expressed in this book are not necessarily those of the publisher.

Unless otherwise indicated, Bible quotations are taken from The New King James Version. Copyright © 1982 by Thomas Nelson, Inc. Used by permission; The New American Standard Bible® (NASB). Copyright © 1960, 1962, 1963, 1968, 1971, 1972, 1973, 1975, 1977, 1995 by The Lockman Foundation. Used by permission; and The HOLY BIBLE, NEW INTERNATIONAL VERSION®. NIV®. Copyright © 1973, 1978, 1984 by International Bible Society. Used by permission of Zondervan.

www.xulonpress.com

Contents

A Glimpse of Eternity	11
Aftershock	22
Root Cause of Pain	31
Poisonous Seeds	39
Your Beliefs Determine Your Path	50
Eternal Consequence	57
Hope for the Future	68
Abide in Christ	75
Jesus Is Our High Priest	84
Live Life Victoriously	89
A Servant's Heart	96

Dedications

I have written this book in honor of my Lord and Savior, Jesus Christ, my Adonai to whom I owe all that I have and all that I am. Jesus has given me a life of joy in exchange for hopelessness and despair. He provided a second opportunity to live with a multitude of promises to guarantee a beautiful future. I am filled with gratitude for the compassion, grace and mercy He has bestowed upon me, especially since it is so undeserved. I hope to share with you His healing power of love and His desire to transform your life into greatness.

To my husband, Rodney: I am grateful to be your chosen bride. God has given me the perfect companion in you. I appreciate the godly guidance you give to me and our family.

To my precious children: may you know the love of God and walk in freedom all the days of your life. May your lives be enriched and led by the power of the Holy Spirit. I declare that your steps are directed and established by the Lord and His blessings are poured out upon you so that you can't contain them. You are a true gift from above. I feel honored to have been chosen by God to be your mother. You have brought me more joy than I could ever express.

To my family: it is truly a privilege to be a part of you. You have given me a heritage in which to be proud. Your never wavering loyalty has made me the person I am today. Thank you for your continual love and support. I appreciate you for allowing me to share our pain in the hope that others may be healed.

Opening Prayer

❦

Oh, my precious heavenly Father, I come to you in the name of Jesus Christ through the power of the blood that was shed on the cross.

Lord, I thank You for all that You have done; I thank You for Your magnificent ways; I thank You for all that You are; I thank You for Your grace, Your mercy, Your unconditional love and Your faithfulness to never leave us nor forsake us. You are great and mighty, and there is none like You. You are the great I AM and there is none above You. I pray that you give to everyone who reads this the ears to hear, the eyes to see and a heart that is receptive to the truth.

I believe and declare that all who choose to have faith in You will be set free from all that is keeping them bound, from every addiction, bad habit and root of destruction. I speak total and complete restoration to their souls, and may Your perfect Spirit from above dwell in them to perfect the work You have begun. Deliver all who are oppressed and set free those who are being held captive.

May all come to see You for who You are, and may they experience Your closeness in the way You originally intended them to enjoy. I ask that Your Spirit be poured out upon them from the top of their head to the tips of their toes.

I pray they may know that You are here and that You are willing and able to do more than that which exceeds their expectations. You will meet their heart's desire. You are the great and mighty Yahweh, the One who heals, restores, and makes all things brand new.

May You make each life brand new in Christ Jesus. I ask that You do these things for one purpose — that You may be lifted up that all men will be drawn unto You in order to further Your kingdom. We give You the glory, the honor, and the praise that You are so worthy to receive.

Amen.

CHAPTER ONE

A Glimpse of Eternity

On the last day of September in 1985 I contemplated a drastic decision to change my destiny. It was a typical warm fall day in West Texas and was during a segment in time which my elders had pronounced as my "best years." However, I did not comprehend what the phrase meant because I definitely was not experiencing the "time of my life." I sat through my high school classes in a daze and was thoroughly convinced there had to be more to life than what I was living.

On one hand, I understood that I was young and had my whole life ahead of me to live, and on the other hand, I believed that age didn't dictate my emotional well being. As a person gets older they gain more knowledge, experience, and maturity, but I didn't believe that those things would heal or take away the anguish on the inside of me.

Bound by chains of loneliness and despair, surrounded by silent tears and an internal cry that never stopped, my life had absolutely nothing I wanted. I felt so much guilt and shame because I knew I had a great family and a decent life, but it wasn't enough. I desired more, much more! I needed to feel love on the inside of me, to look in the mirror and know that what I saw was good and not just one big screw-up.

My internal agony was so overwhelming that I was unable to see anything positive in my life or in the lives of others. As I would watch those around me, I would see them laugh and smile and yet it was hard for me to believe they were truly happy on the inside. If they were truly happy, then what was so wrong with me? Why was I not able to receive or give this happiness? I understood that laughter comes and goes, but joy is found in the stillness of your soul. This was a stillness I had never known, yet yearned for every day.

In my eyes, meaningful or intimate communication with the people in my life on any level was impossible. I was not able to sit down and make myself vulnerable by sharing my inner-most thoughts. When I made an attempt to do this, I felt misunderstood or perceived I was being told how wrong I was because I didn't see things the way they did. I desperately tried to communicate the fact that something needed to change. I would throw little hints or big hints, but the response was seemingly superficial and definitely not what I wanted or believed I needed. I had reached out in every way I knew possible, always reaching for acceptance and reaching to be understood and reaching for someone to care about how I felt.

I learned you are either right or wrong and any different perspective was considered wrong. I didn't understand that righteousness is the guideline, not personal views of right and wrong.

I longed for true intimacy, needing to sense a connection with someone. I felt so alone and isolated. I wanted someone to care about my thoughts and my desires. I was desperate to feel significant and it was crucial for me to know that my very existence was important.

For several years I attempted to make myself happy by experimenting with substances that appeared to bring joy to others. Other people would laugh, joke, and have a great time when alcohol was involved, so I thought that it would give me the same results. Most of us have experienced the temporary "fun" that happens in the moments of a party, but then the sun comes up nothing is different. It is proven that alcohol and drugs only bring temporary relief and are definitely not an instant fix to a bad day. There is no question that the "party lifestyle" breeds destruction to a damaged soul, and it without doubt causes endless pain and guilt. We call it fun, but it eventually brings on more depression and self-hatred. After a few years of dabbling in the deceptive ploy of the worldly tactics which are filled with lies and false hope, I realized there was no amount of alcohol or drugs could end or take away my misery.

I would reflect on myself as a person and analyze my actions. I knew I wasn't anywhere close to being perfect, but I felt as though I was a good person with a good heart. I tried to put other's concerns before my own and I viewed myself as a giving, caring and kind individual who liked to laugh and have fun. I wasn't confrontational or argumentative and was fairly easy to get along with most of the time. I tried to have somewhat of a positive perspective about life and situations.

I know this sounds contradictory to what I usually felt because I was so confused. I saw myself as a decent person, but I thought there was no way I could have a positive outlook on my life because I was so empty and emotionally wounded. I didn't feel I belonged and felt like an outcast who was different from everyone else. I didn't feel that I was wanted or even belonged in my family.

My father didn't live with me and there were times he would call and ask to speak to one of my siblings. Knowing he was on the phone, I would get so excited about talking to him! I would anxiously run to the phone and patiently wait at the kitchen bar for my turn to talk. Then, I would hear

"O.K. I'll tell her," and click, they would hang up the phone. I would fight back the tears as they would tell me he had to go back to work, but he wanted me to know he would talk to me later. This happened so many times and I saw clearly how my siblings would make excuses for him. I just didn't understand why my father would talk to the others, but not want to talk to me.

I believe my father was oblivious to how I felt and he thought it was no big deal. To me, however, it was just conformation that something had to be desperately wrong with me as a person for my brothers and sisters to receive acceptance and I was left to feel like a nuisance. My hurt turned into inward anger and I began to hate myself. I felt my pain was never validated and I believed my family didn't care how I felt. I perceived that I was not important enough for them to be concerned with my emotions or perspective. In my diligent pursuit of happiness, I ended up emptier than when I had begun.

Desperation and hopelessness became my way of life, so on that autumn day in September of 1985, I was walking home from school and was consumed with internal sorrow. I finally decided to take action into my own hands. I believed I had nowhere to turn and was convinced that no one truly understood.

When the school day came to an end, I went home and got on my knees and cried out to God like never before. It was a cry of desperation and a cry for forgiveness.

I had been to church on and off my whole life, yet I didn't really know anything about God. Still, there was one thing I believed - He was a forgiving God. I believed that if I cried out for forgiveness, He would forgive me, so I asked for forgiveness on what I was about to do.

Sitting on my bedroom floor and crying out to God, I reached under my bed and pulled out a spiral notebook to write a letter to the ones I loved. I was asking them to forgive me. Despair overwhelmed me because I knew that nobody would ever grasp my actions. Yet the anguish of my heart's wailing and a yearning to be free from the pain that plagued my soul definitely outweighed the sorrow I felt for them. Tears flowed down my cheeks like rain as I said my final goodbyes to the ones I loved, knowing I would never speak to them again.

Through my continual sobs and the thoughts racing through my mind, I could hear my mom working in the back yard as she often did to keep our house in perfect condition. Our playful little sheltie was barking at the top of her lungs and running around in circles as she chased her tail and everything else in the yard. One would think that this pleasant home atmosphere would keep anyone from becoming destitute. Oh, but nothing could stop the years of anguish I felt and the desperation for an end to the vicious cycle of inward agony which was finally coming to a close.

I came out of my room, peeked down the hall and hurriedly walked across the house so no one would see me and try to cancel my mission. I was determined to stop the pain! I swiftly walked into my parent's bedroom, knelt beside my mother's side of the bed and slowly reached into her nightstand to pull out her thirty-eight caliber gun.

My sobs had turned into desperate pleas, pleas to the Maker of the heavens and the earth. I knew about Him because I would often stay at my grandmother's house on weekends and she would speak of the love and forgiveness of her Savior, Jesus Christ. With this small frame of reference, I pleaded for forgiveness for what I was about to do. I also believed I would receive that forgiveness.

My cry to the heavens never stopped as I went into the bathroom and locked the door, saying over and over, *"GOD FORGIVE ME, GOD FORGIVE ME, GOD, PLEASE FORGIVE ME!"* I stepped into the shower while continuing my distressed plea. I knelt down on my knees and placed the gun to my head. Bringing my sobs under control, I took a deep breath and then calmly asked Jesus for forgiveness one last time.

A still, small voice told me to remove the gun from my head and place it at my chest. I argued with this voice and told it I was determined for it to be over and I wasn't going to take the chance of this not working. The still, small voice replied ever so gently and explained to me that it would be easier on my family to find me this way and that I wouldn't miss because I knew the exact location of my heart.

I saw a rapid flash, a vision of the way I would look with a bullet through my head. There would be pieces of my tissue splattered along the wall and half of my face would be gone. Permanent damage would be unbearable to live with if for some bizarre reason I survived. Then I saw another vision of myself with a puddle of blood on the floor around me. I had compassion for the humiliation and shock my family was about to experience and I desired to make it as painless for them as I could, although nothing about this whole situation was going to be easy.

Cautiously, I placed the gun on the left side of my chest and pointed it straight for my heart. Gently placing my finger on the trigger, and before I pulled it, the gun ignited with a sudden discharge. Instantly, I felt the piercing burn of the bullet as it passed through my chest and immediately I felt the rushing of blood beginning to fill my lungs. I knew it was only a matter of time before I would feel no more pain and see eternity. My goal had been accomplished!

I laid back into the shower realizing time no longer existed. My eyesight slowly dimmed until blindness blotted out the last few seconds of my world. Staring into the blackness with my blinded eyes, I heard the faint sounds of my barking dog finally vanish. I had become blind and deaf. Breathing in my last breath, I closed my eyes as death gripped my soul.

As I left my body, I began traveling faster than the speed of light and my entire being was plagued with the sensation of falling. Helplessness overtook me as I kept falling and falling and falling! I was no longer in control of my destiny and there was nothing I could do that would stop this horrid falling sensation.

Suddenly, an indescribable explosion of indescribable pain erupted on the inside of me. It was like someone took acid and poured it over the top of my head until it ran over every inch of my body! If that was not torturous enough, it seemed like a massive high pressured hose sprayed the acid to make sure it hit every molecule of my being. No human has ever come even close to experiencing this kind of pain; it was agony in its purest form! That terrifying burning sensation cannot be expressed in words and it was a pain so fierce that it had no earthly correlation.

I had entered ultimate darkness, a darkness so black that you couldn't see an object if it were on the tip of your nose. There was absolutely no light.

My agonizing cry for forgiveness turned into a hideous, violent scream as I burned with an unquenchable acidic fire that is beyond expression. It was at that exact moment that I realized I was banished completely and eternally from the presence of the one true God!

I realized my soul had been transformed into a being of sin and death. I had actually become total sin and my eyes were opened to the fact that sin is a state of being, not just an act. I became everything that God the Father is not: I was the complete opposite of God's character, I had nothing good within me and I turned into the opposite of love - a being of total fear.

Wrenching loneliness surrounded me as I looked across the fiery pit and saw hundreds upon hundreds of souls (too many to count) just like me and all were screaming in agony. Each one was a formless being begging for another chance, yet *NEVER* to receive one. Although we were right next to each other, we were forbidden to communicate. We were together, yet we were in total isolation from one another.

My knowledge was made perfect. Revelation of truth and pure wisdom became a part of me. I no longer had questions because infinite knowledge of life, creation, and all of existence down to the last detail was known to all. Yet, the only information that was of any importance was the fact that Jesus Christ is Lord for eternity. Truly nothing else mattered and we all knew that *it is all about Him.* We understood that the purpose of life itself had been to bring honor and glory to Jesus Christ. That was it – it was that simple!

As I looked into the eyes of each one, I viewed their entire soul. There was one person who was looking back at me, and it was understood that we had lived our life in blindness to the fact that Jesus Christ was and is the true living God and there shall be no other gods before Him. Nothing in anyone's heart should take His rightful place. We knew we were in this place because we were foolish and chose not to hear and do what was right according to God's word. We had made this choice out of deceit, yet the effect of our ignorance was eternal, never to end.

There were no secrets; everyone knew everything there was to know about me and I knew everything about them. I looked upon this one particular individual and I knew everything - not one sin or action was hidden. I knew the family lineage, background, everything this person had ever done wrong, every sin which was committed and all the sorrow which was experienced. There was nothing hidden about anyone's life in this place and every secret was revealed.

The others also knew everything about me, as well - every sin I had committed. Everything I had ever done was out there for all to see and know. Complete transparency of minds, emotions, and wills were revealed from the beginning to the end of everyone's life on earth. Souls were turned inside out and there were no physical bodies to cover or hide the real you.

It was mutual among every person there that they wanted no one else to enter such torment. They would look out with pure sorrow and beg for the people on earth to understand and seek truth in order not to join them.

I saw many different chambers; however, my movement was restricted as I tried to turn and look to see the details. Behind me was an indescribable creature with dragon-like heads upon his body, and he stood more fierce than anything the earth has ever seen. I was only allowed to see a glimpse of him and for that I am grateful — no eyes have ever seen such a terrifying sight. Although I could scarcely see him, I could feel his presence which was made up of intense and violent fear. There was so much more I wasn't allowed to look upon. No words in the human vocabulary could possibly describe this place I was in, the place the Bible describes as Hell.

I now had become nothing but a formless, tormented soul who consisted of everything as hideous as you can imagine. Loneliness was no longer in me, it *was* me. Hurt, bitterness, anger, murder, lies, complete shame and guilt was all a part of who I had become. Fear and everything else that is evil pervaded me.

As my screams and cries continued calling out from the darkness, I looked out across the vast expanse and saw all three heavens. I also saw the universe in its entirety. We think it is so large, but it is actually very small compared to the other areas of existence. I saw the great gulf that separates the heavens and the vast deep that has no end. As I looked upon our universe and saw what we call earth, it was magnified as if it was enlarged through a magnifying glass.

All creation far surpasses our sight and touch and is absolutely beyond human vocabulary or comprehension. The three heavens were separated by an expanse of nothingness, which was like a massive river or elongated ocean with no flowing water. The enormous distance between them is larger than the size of our universe. Yet, it is just a simple dividing line for God, a completely dark, colorless void. God is so massive and incredible; I pray that He will reveal to you how majestic He really is.

After I viewed all that I was allowed to see, I looked up and saw a huge massive hand that was brighter than any light you can imagine, and it reached down, scooped me up and instantly whisked me away from all torment.

I began traveling over the expanse again, faster than the speed of light, and I came to the heaven where the God of all Creation dwells. This is the place we all desire to go when we leave this earth. Love consumed me as I was now in the presence of the true and living God. This was a habitat of pure love and a place of perfection. Our dreams can never grasp the greatness and awesomeness of the reality of eternal beauty. With my pain and suffering far behind me, I found myself complete and whole, instantly washed from head to toe. The glory there is too exquisite for words. I was not allowed to stay or see anything in detail; I could only travel over it for I was just passing through.

I was able to experience the pure beauty of the one true and holy God who is so brilliant that once you are in His presence you realize He is truly what you've been longing for. The colors were so bright and refreshing that their very sight was rejuvenating and full of energy. There was an overwhelming sense of peace, joy, and complete serenity. I was engulfed in absolute truth and didn't want to leave. I received the revelation that I belonged in God's presence!

Not given a choice, I left heaven and again watched the expanse pass by in front of me. I crossed over the universe which brought me back through the galaxies into earth's atmosphere. I could recognize it from afar. Since the spiritual world is not bound to physical laws, I entered through the roof of my home and was gently placed back into my physical body. Instantly, I could see and hear again! I opened my eyes just in time to see the vessel of my Lord go up and vanish as He passed through the ceiling.

As I laid there in total shock and awe of what I had just experienced, I realized that just a few minutes ago, before the gun went off, I had felt hopeless and had no desire to live. Now I was full of hope, knowing I could face whatever came my way. Not only was I simply capable of living, but I now had a *desire* to live. At that moment, I knew I had a responsibility to tell all of God's people how real Hell is and yet how much our God loves us. Never in my wildest dreams could I know how difficult this would be to accomplish and how hard my enemy would fight to keep me from fulfilling my one true obligation.

I knew I had been given the strength to endure the situation I was facing. I now knew the truth that Jesus is Lord and I immediately accepted Him into my heart and became born again.

The inside of me had been changed, not just because I had an out-of-body experience, but because Jesus now lived in me. Somehow, someway I knew in the innermost part of my being that everything was going to be alright.

CHAPTER TWO

Aftershock

Mother came in from the backyard and I could hear her walking through the living room. "Mom, Mom!" I called.

"Where are you?" she wanted to know.

"In your bathroom," I calmly called out.

Seconds later I heard the door handle jiggle. My mom replied with a puzzled voice "The door is locked, are you ok?"

My response was one she never could have expected, "You need to call an ambulance, I shot myself."

Confused and shocked she yelled "YOU WHAT, OH MY GOD, YOU WHAT?" Hysteria struck as she ran to get the phone and call 911. In a panic she rushed to the garage and grabbed a sledge hammer to bust the door open.

Shock, disbelief and fear gripped my mother's face as she saw her baby girl lying on the floor in a puddle of blood with a gun in her hand. Not knowing what to do or say she frantically walked out of the room but returned quickly with the paramedics. Cautiously, they reached for the gun as they made a rapid assessment of my physical condition. They believed my life was fading quickly and didn't waste

Delivered

a second placing me on the gurney. My mom was standing next to me as they were rolling me toward the ambulance and I looked up at her and said, "Mom, everything is going to be alright."

Hysterically she yelled "NO, IT'S NOT, YOU'RE DYING!"

My body was grayish in color and I had the pallor of death, but what nobody knew was that I had already met death and now had been given a second chance at life.

When we got to the driveway my step- dad had just pulled up to the curb and my mom began explaining everything. The EMS personnel looked at the ambulance driver and said, "We'd better go *if* we are going!" They were convinced I was dying and that more than likely I wouldn't make it to the hospital.

Amazed that I survived the trip and knowing they didn't have a moment to spare, the ER team rushed me into a room and began working quickly. One of the first steps was a surgical knife ripping a hole in my skin between my ribs. With no anesthetic, they jabbed a tube in the incision and punctured my lung to drain it from all the blood. The x-rays revealed that the bullet missed my heart by less than one-quarter of an inch. It ricocheted off one of my ribs and exploded. It left many fragments in my body, but the main part of the bullet exited out my back.

I was told that the impact of a .38 revolver at such close range should have exploded my heart or done a lot more damage, and there was no way I should be alive much less be in such a stable physical state. I don't know much about guns, but I do know it was only by a true miracle that I was alive.

I was bewildered at the comments the ER team made about me while they were coming in and out of the room to treat me. One lady said "My goodness girl, with a body like that there is no reason for a gun, honey. Use that thing to get what you want."

Another one responded by saying, "Shoot, if I looked like that there is nothing I couldn't have."

One of the guys said, "If I could have a piece of that, mmmmm, well life's good just think' in about it."

Laying there naked with barely a sheet to cover me I was ashamed, embarrassed, and wondering if they thought I was supposed to be flattered. How could people be so cold and insensitive during an emergency situation? There I was, in the process of a blood transfusion with a bullet in my chest, several tubes coming out of my body and the medical help was making sexual innuendoes. I allowed the superficial mindset of people to get me frustrated.

My family was outside in the emergency room waiting in utter shock and in total confusion from this whole experience. Never could they ever imagine I would do something like this. Most of them thought it had to be an outside negative influence because the "happy-go-lucky" girl they knew was not capable of acting so drastic.

Once the emergency room doctors performed the essential medical procedures, they took me to the intensive care unit. I was weak but coherent during the entire process. In a matter of a few minutes the ICU specialist determined I was stable enough to go to a regular room.

In a few short hours my assessment progressed from she is dying and will not survive to she is completely fine and the only thing physically wrong is her wound and a few broken ribs. Only a supernatural God can change a tragedy into a miracle!

When you try to take your life, most people think you are crazy and weird. I was neither of these because I believed I was just emotionally crushed beyond repair. I was simply a person who wanted a life without continual heartache, a life without feeling emotionally abandoned and a person who simply needed a vision of hope.

I know there was a very strong and peaceful presence about me because one doesn't come away from the presence of God without having people notice. However, this presence is foreign to most people and therefore unrecognizable. Years later, a family member confessed to me that they thought this presence around me was demonic, yet it wasn't long before they discovered it was truly the presence of God and the unexplainable peace of God.

My recovery continued to be quick and miraculous. I remember many times in the middle of the night when my doctor would pull a chair beside my bed and silently stare at me in disbelief. He knew there was no medical reason to explain why I was alive, so he just sat and wondered quietly. If this man hadn't believed in miracles before, I knew he did now.

By law, anyone who attempts suicide has to meet with a psychiatrist. Therefore, the one on call automatically became my doctor. My first experience was quite interesting to say the least. He abruptly walked into my room, grabbed a chair and dropped it near the foot of my bed. Just as fast he sat down, he looked at me and said, "So why did ya do it?" Can you believe that? And what was even more amazing was that he actually expected me to respond. I have never in my life experienced such a heartless individual. How in the world could he think that I would ever open up my fragile, bleeding heart and soul to that kind of behavior? It was obvious I was even having difficulty opening up to people who actually acted like they cared. He could have at least introduced himself before being so rude.

I fought back the tears as I turned my head away from him and realized that my emotional recovery was up to me and me alone. My family had no idea how to handle this; what family really does? I knew my emotional recovery would be like a long journey that would possibly isolate me from the understanding of those around me. Still, it was a journey I was willing to take because I knew I wasn't isolated from the healing power of love that would never leave me – the love of Jesus. I knew He understood my pain, and

I knew that somehow and in some way He would see me through the persecution I would have to endure.

In my parent's desperation, they cried out to God with a different request. They pleaded that Jesus would save their baby girl because all they knew was that their daughter had shot herself and had virtually no chance of survival. My stepfather went into the same room where I had obtained the gun and fell to his knees. There he begged God and told Him that he would do anything if He would just save his baby girl. He said that he would even serve God completely and wholeheartedly for the rest of his life if only He would grant him this one thing. As the Lord heard his cry and desperate plea, heavenly love was poured all over him. As a result, my step-dad invited Jesus to be the Lord of his life.

After this experience, my step-dad came to me in the hospital and brought me a plaque of "Footprints in the Sand." To this day, I look at it often to remind myself of where I have been and where I am headed. He told me he would take me to church anywhere I wanted to go, but I shouldn't tell mom because he didn't think she was ready for that.

Little did he know that my mom had also been on her knees in the bedroom and had completely given her life to Jesus Christ as well! It was a decision she would never regret. I told my step-dad of a church I had seen in a vision - the church I knew we were supposed to attend. A new life was beginning for all of us and not just for me.

My hospital room was filled with many flowers and gifts from friends and family who wanted me to know that they cared. Although I felt their concern and generosity, it seemed a little superficial. Now that I was in a tragic situation, everyone was willing to say they were there for me. Strangely, just yesterday it appeared to me that they were shunning me or giving me the cold shoulder.

True friends are able to be honest with one another, sharing thoughts, feelings, and experiences without judgment. True friends are loyal and trustworthy. I believe time revealed who my true friends really were, and I am forever grateful for the few who stood by my side in complete support. I came to believe that one must learn how to be a true friend inside the family unit before becoming that genuine friend on the outside. Real friends help each other weather the storm even if they get hurt in the process.

I was told that my father had jumped on the first flight possible after hearing the tragic news about me, his youngest daughter. He arrived at the hospital the next day asking if I could go to live with him. My mom gave me the choice, but I somehow knew that moving wasn't the solution so I chose to stay.

My older sisters and other family members really couldn't identify with me, nor did they know what to do. Basically, all they did individually was to express their concern by saying, "You know I'm here for you." Everything was viewed as my problem, and no one ever took responsibility for any actions or words which may have led me down the wrong path. I don't deny I was in this spot by my own doing, but the inner hurts which compelled me also came from my response to other people's actions.

For the most part, everyone kept their distance because they considered me to be a severe mental case and that my condition was somehow contagious. They ignored the reality, somehow hoping time would just make it go away. All of this served to once again remind me that I was all alone on my journey to recovery. I had no choice but to trust Jesus Christ to show me a new way and a new life, a life of joy in the midst of my problems.

I wanted my family to sit down with me and listen to my hurts, listen to where I was emotionally and to understand why I was there. Then I expected them to do something about their actions and my problems. I didn't want them to put misguided blame on me for running with the wrong crowd. I wanted my family to be able to communicate on an intimate level until they understood every detail.

I never received the response I wanted, and I have come to understand that regardless of how others respond or don't respond, I am accountable for what is on the inside of me. Absolutely no one can care or love me like Jesus. He is the only one who can restore a broken soul.

A few weeks after leaving the hospital, I returned to my cardiologist's office for a follow-up visit. He told my mom and me that we didn't owe him any fee for his service because in his mind he did nothing for me. I had been in the hospital for about a week or so, and he just threw the bill away. Of course, it had been an enormous fee. He knew we had no insurance coverage, and he said he didn't feel right making us pay when he knew he didn't have anything to do with my recovery. I believe this was his way of confessing that my healing was an undeniable miracle!

By law I was to continue to see a psychiatrist for my emotional issues, so I went back to the stone-cold doctor who I'd seen in the hospital. The visit in his office went about the same as it did in my hospital room - terrible. It appeared that this man could have cared less about what was going on with me; in fact, it seemed as though he was just working "on the clock." His solution was to dope me up and make me lethargic. I didn't need drugs to sedate me; I needed a solution to fix my inward pain. I knew my parents and family cared because they were related, but I didn't think they liked me as a person.

My mom took me back for my second visit to the psychiatrist, and as we were sitting in the waiting room she asked me if I wanted to leave. Of course I said yes! Her conclusion was, "You don't need him — you have Jesus." I agreed, so we left. I was relieved in many ways, yet I was also scared because I knew I needed help in understanding my emotions and thoughts. I also believed that it just wasn't me who needed help - it was my family as well.

Now, I wouldn't recommend this to everyone! God has given mental health professionals a tremendous amount of knowledge, and there are times when it is absolutely essential that someone take medication for depression or for other reasons. There are chemical imbalances in the body which do affect many things and sometimes medicine is needed. At this point in my life, however, medicine was not necessary. I was no longer a threat to myself, nor had I ever been a threat to anyone else. I was a changed person. Although there was an enormous amount of healing that needed to take place within me, I knew that the medicine would make me numb. I didn't want to be numb; I wanted to be whole! True emotional healing can only be found through the one remedy which many doctors don't recognize. That remedy is the word of God.

When I say I believed my family needed help, I mean that they needed to be taught how to communicate in a healthy manner and to understand the cause of their own pain and oppression. This is important because we all give out what is on the inside of ourselves because we don't understand anything else. The criticism, emotional abandonment, and other mistreatment that they received in their lives eventually became a part of their behavior. This is why we often end up doing the very things we hate. We haven't recognized the source of these actions and feelings, so we haven't changed the direction of the path we walk. I am so grateful that my family has now been taught the road to truth.

Most of my family members have received salvation, and for those who haven't developed a personal relationship with Christ there is continual intercession in prayer on their behalf. God is faithful, and I declare that my household and my entire family — every name —will be written in the

Lamb's Book of Life; not one will miss out; all will be a part of the kingdom of God.

Each one of us has a solitary road to walk at our own individual speed which allows restoration and maturity to take place. I have learned real maturity doesn't come by getting older; it is in the process of taking on righteous responsibility. This can be characterized as doing what is right in the eyes of God simply because it is the right thing to do and by bringing our thoughts and emotions in line with obedience to the One who sits on the throne. We choose to love regardless of the circumstances.

Like most people, my expectation of God was distorted. I understood the sovereignty of God, so it was difficult for me to understand why He didn't just take away all my inner pain in an instant. Isn't that what makes us question His love for us? Instead of questioning Him, we must understand that healing, whether it be spiritual, mental, emotional or physical, is a choice.

Living in freedom is a choice, and there is a price to pay for that freedom. If we always received our answers as soon as we prayed for them, then the Scriptures about counting the cost or having faith would have no real meaning. There is a definite cost associated with victory, and I was willing to pay that cost. Little did I know that my own willingness to obey God would take me through years of agonizing sorrow.

CHAPTER THREE

Root Cause of Pain

*I*n order for God to completely heal me inside and out, it was essential for me to understand the root cause of all my problems and pain and how that root took hold in my heart.

Emotional pain comes in many different forms and levels of intensity. Unfortunately, all of us have to experience the "pains" of life to different degrees, yet one thing is for certain: there is coming a day when there will be no more pain, there will be no more suffering and we will bask in the presence of pure wholeness!

I know that God heals people in different ways. Sometimes this is done instantly, and other times it takes a little longer.

There are also situations when the journey is long in order to receive the fullness of freedom. I have experienced many different healing time frames in my life, but one thing is guaranteed. God will heal those who diligently seek Him.

But without faith it is impossible to please him: for he that cometh to God must believe that he is, and that he is a rewarder of them that diligently seek him.

Hebrews 11:6 KJV

Like most people who suffer from deep-rooted emotional pain, my brokenness began at a very young age. I have two older sisters and one big brother. My parents divorced when I was four years old, and I'll never forget leaving the house where we had lived! As I looked out the back window of the car, the picture of my father standing at the front door with tears in his eyes is frozen in my mind. My oldest sister and brother stood next to him. The tension I sensed was so strong that I knew something was wrong, but I didn't know what it was. My other sister and I were the only ones in the car and I wondered why the others weren't coming with us. I didn't understand all the sadness and confusion. I just remember feeling it!

Divorce leaves families shattered and broken in tremendous ways. I don't know anyone who is a part of a broken family who hasn't had a lot of emotional junk to overcome. This just isn't the way God intended it to be! Nevertheless, it happens every day and we need to learn how to triumph over our childhood ailments and disappointments. It is so important that we learn to conquer and overcome our problems so we can fulfill the purpose intended for our lives.

The family unit was designed by God right from the beginning with Adam and Eve. Consider the major issues the first family had to overcome. Eve convinced her husband to disobey God and look at the results. Whew! There was marital conflict from the start! One blamed the other and the other blamed the serpent for their disobedience. Both refused to take responsibility for their actions. We see their children having great rivalry, and the jealous friction and anger between the two brothers was so great that it led to one of them killing the other. Throughout history you can see difficult family challenges, yet God is all about family.

Many of God's people, whose lives are recorded in the Bible, faced great pain and suffering because of their families. Christ himself suffered in the family unit. Scripture tells us He was born out of wedlock and without an earthly Father, and was raised by a step-father. He was rejected by not only His siblings, but by most of His race and His actions were completely misunderstood by a majority of the people of His time. Jesus suffered all things for all mankind and He continues to take on our suffering when we ask Him to help us. I have learned that just because you *go* through problems, it doesn't mean you must *suffer* through them. In other words, you can have peace in the midst of your storms.

Soon after my parents divorced, my mom remarried and my siblings remained split by the court system. At that time it was unusual for children to be taken from their mother in a divorce. Now it is much more common. Staying with my mother, I had to move to a different city and didn't get to see my father very often. No one explained anything about the divorce to me, but then again, it probably would have been difficult because I was just four. Even as I got older, life was just assumed, not understood.

Having a step-father in the home was new to me, and confusion was definitely part of the equation. A short period of time went by and all I really knew was that I had a new dad. One day I just started calling him Dad because I thought that he was my new dad. This just melted his heart. Those of you who are step-parents and have this type of relationship with your step-children know what I'm talking about. I didn't mean to belittle my father at all and I stilled loved him just as much, but I just thought it was the right thing to do. I now had two dads: the old dad who lived with my siblings and the new dad who lived with me. It seemed simple enough, right? Boy, was I in for some long, hard life lessons.

I know now that it must have absolutely crushed my father to know that I was now calling another man "Dad." At that age I didn't know any difference and my relationship with my step-father was great. He loved me as if I was his own child, and he still does. He adopted all of my mom's children into his heart and has loved us with a true father's love without any intentions of taking my father's place in our lives. Nobody can ever fill the void or take the place of a natural parent. Also, I now realize that the relationship I was building with my step-dad caused a tremendous amount of conflict between my mother and father.

My relationship with my father was very distant. For this reason, I want to encourage all divorced or unwed parents to set aside your own hurt and negative opinion about each other. Make provision for your children to have and maintain their own relationship with each of you. Mothers, choose to nurture your children in love and forgiveness instead of bitterness and division. Fathers, choose not to abandon your God-given responsibility of parenthood, as it is a separate relationship from your former mate. Your children need you and your guidance, not your absence. Remember, it is never about the child support; it is about relationship.

One of the things that came between my father and me was parent rivalry. The damage was already done long before the wrong was recognized or admitted. A broken home leaves children battling with security, acceptance and self-esteem.

I remember one time when I was about five when I went to visit my father in El Paso, Texas, where I was born. He explained that we were going to spend the day with a female friend of his. I was so excited that my father was including me in something! There had been such a void in my heart since we left him, and just being with him brought me so much joy. The day was going to be a great father-daughter day with a friend. I remember feeling so special that I couldn't quit smiling.

Unfortunately, his friend wasn't as excited to see me as I was to meet her. As a matter of fact, she was quite ticked off, to say the least. I remember him introducing me to her and I was shocked at her response! She did say hello to me, but it was not a good hello at all because it was followed by the screamed words, "WHAT IS SHE DOING HERE?" She took my father into the other room and let him have it. She wanted to know why I was there and why they weren't spending the day alone. I felt so ashamed for being there since it was pretty obvious I wasn't wanted. She didn't try to hide her feelings at all; she wanted nothing to do with me and was very expressive about it.

After my father calmed her down they walked out of the bedroom with a little baby in a carrier and all of us left. I remember riding in the back seat of the car wishing I wasn't there. I wanted to be with my father, but I knew my presence was causing him problems. I remember thinking that if I would not have been there, my father and this lady would have been better off. My insecurities concerning my father began to grow because he was never there for me and I knew it wasn't good for me to be around him either. My lack of understanding deeply hurt my feelings, but I was too scared to say anything. It turned out that the little baby who was with my dad and his friend was really my step-brother.

I had enjoyed such a good relationship with my step-dad that I just assumed it would be that way with my step-mom. I tried so very hard for her to like me. I tried being really nice to her, and I did my best never to get into trouble, but no matter what I did she couldn't stand me.

One day I thought, "Well, I have two dads and now I have two moms, so the right thing to do is to call my step-mom, Mom. Boy, what a mistake that was! I remember that we were in the bathroom getting dressed and I looked at her and called her Mom. You would have thought I burned the house down! She just freaked out and started screaming at me, "DON'T YOU EVER CALL ME THAT. I AM NOT YOUR MOTHER!" My father came running into the room and asked what was going on. When she told him, he very patiently took me in his arms and tried to calm her down at the same time.

The rejection I kept facing with my step-mom was absolutely crushing me, and I couldn't figure out why I was so disgusting to her. This was truly the beginning of all my insecurities. Seeds of rejection were planted deep within my heart by a father who no longer was there and a step-mother who hated me for no particular reason.

Rejection can be one of the most damaging emotions to experience. It is felt on different levels and has a multitude of negative effects depending on the closeness of the relationship. When a child experiences rejection or abuse from a parent, it is truly one of the greatest challenges to overcome. Look at our prison system — it is full of people who have been rejected, abused and mistreated mainly by their fathers. God created an undeniable, supernatural connection between fathers and their children. You see this in every walk of life and all around the world.

My observation has been that most children who are extremely rebellious usually don't have a good relationship with their father. I could go on and on about the horrible effects that broken parent-child relationships have on us and we are reminded every day when we see the crime and drug use that goes on around us.

It wasn't that my father totally rejected me, but my interpretation of his actions spoke this to me. I was a young child who didn't understand adult situations and I was not supposed to be able to understand the pressures of being an adult.

Time went on, and my relationship with my step-mother just continued to spiral downward. Whenever I went on vacation to see them, I would become physically ill from the stress of knowing that I wasn't wanted and I couldn't do anything about it. In all fairness, I believed my father wanted me; it just appeared that he didn't have time for me. Either way, I felt rejected. Either he was working or busy doing activities with the other kids, and I felt I was just there to go along for the ride and be in the background. It seemed as though everything was about someone else. When you are a small child you need to know that you are important. There were two concepts I questioned continually: my importance and my own self-worth.

Generally life teaches us to move forward and not look back at the past. For most of us that means ignoring both the nagging memories and the unresolved pains that haunt us. We live in a state of denial, hiding behind busy schedules, emotional binging and the inability to get alone and sit quiet. We should learn to be still before God and allow Him to take control of our past and let Him wash it away never to be remembered again. Jesus came to deliver us from our past, set us free from all oppression and give us a future.

> **Brothers, I do not consider myself to have taken hold of it. But one thing I do: Forgetting what is behind and straining toward what is ahead ....**
> **Philippians 3:13 NIV**

So often we assume that our family knows we love them and yet we don't really examine our actions or words to see if we really express or communicate love. We can be guilty of taking one another for granted and we forget what a few simple words of encouragement can do. All of us should take a close look at ourselves to see what we are communicating to those who are closest to us. Is it love or something carried over from our own inward baggage?

When you are a parent of more than one child, it is essential that you make each child feel special. That can be so challenging because each child is different in personality and needs. We must be very sensitive to pick up on their insecurities in the beginning so that their afflictions don't grow and eventually overtake them.

That "overtaking" is what happened to me. I allowed my feelings of insignificance to control my life and thoughts. I didn't know any better so I didn't understand that you make a choice as to how you view yourself regardless of how you think others view you.

CHAPTER FOUR
Poisonous Seeds

*I*f you have been a Christian for any length of time, you have probably heard teachings on seed time and harvest. God's Word tells us that seed planting is a spiritual principle on which our entire world operates. Just like gardening, you prepare the soil, plant, water and feed. After a little time, voila, you have a product as a result of your work. Naturally the size of your harvest depends on how much you planted, watered and fertilized. In order to be emotionally and mentally whole, you must invest time in planting healthy (Godly) seeds into your life as well as in the lives of others.

I spent most of my time watering and pampering the painful junk which sprang up from the poisonous seeds that were planted in me instead of the seeds of truth. I didn't know any better because I had not been taught, yet the effects from the poisonous seeds were still dreadfully damaging. We have the ability to choose ignorance or wisdom for our lives. A wise man will seek after knowledge of the truth and the truth of the Word of God tells us our words have power.

My people are destroyed for lack of knowledge...
                              Hosea 4:6 NASB

Death and life are in the power of the tongue...
                              Proverbs 18:21 NASB

I believe the words we speak are the most powerful seeds we can ever plant, and speaking is something all of us do throughout the day. According to spiritual principles, we are sowing seeds in our life as well as the lives of others every time we open our mouth.

In Scripture we read about the importance of a blessing being spoken by a father to his children. In the Old Testament, every time a blessing was spoken over a child, that very thing came to pass. Think about it: the father would speak over his children and foretell their future by simply laying his hand on them and saying what was to happen by the power of the Holy Spirit. Amazingly, it actually came to pass every time. We have the ability to speak life into others or we have the ability to speak destruction. The greatest lie ever told was "sticks and stones may break my bones, but words will never hurt me." Words can and will destroy your soul *if you allow them.*

The question is, how do you keep hurtful words from cutting right through you? How can you keep those angry, poisonous words spoken in the middle of an argument from haunting you day and night? The answer is simple: we must choose our own thoughts and perspective. We can't control what thoughts pop into our head, but we can control what we allow to stay. When a bad seed is planted, we must choose to uproot it and toss it out.

I know that when someone says something to me that is harmful, I have the choice to either meditate on the painful words which were spoken and allow them to take root in my heart, or I can make a conscious effort to immediately forgive the other person. In the book of Acts a man named Stephen was stoned for telling the truth. He was completely innocent of any wrongdoing and his response was, "Father, forgive them."

Do you quickly forgive others when you don't feel like forgiving and even when you have been wronged either intentionality or ignorantly from another person? If we don't forgive even the smallest things that are done to us, then the root of unforgiveness takes control on the inside of us and becomes a cancer to our soul. Unforgiveness is a deadly poison that can control our thoughts and actions even when we don't realize it..

Have you ever found yourself having a mental conversation with someone who isn't even present? This doesn't mean you're crazy — it means you're normal because everyone role-plays conversations or events in their head. The real issue to ponder is whether these thoughts are healthy or destructive in nature.

I would sit and daydream about conversations I had which made me feel worthless or unwanted. I would think about them over and over again. You know how it is when you have a conversation with someone and it doesn't really go as you wanted. Later on you say to yourself, "Man, I should have said this or that. If only I would have thought of this to say. How dare they say that to me? The nerve of them!" You can't imagine how they could even think that way. You know what I'm talking about. Before long you find yourself mad all over again!

These conversations can be very destructive. I used to think they were harmless until the Holy Spirit began to reveal to me how they were controlling my emotions and how my emotions were controlling my life.

For example, I would remember how my mom had said to me, "I can't believe you just did that!" when I had just put the ice cream into the refrigerator instead of the freezer.

This was a fairly natural response on her part. In fact, I couldn't believe I had done it either because I just wasn't paying attention. However, I would take that statement and begin thinking that she was right and why I had done such a stupid thing. My thoughts were, "I can't do anything right; I can't even put away the ice cream! I am pretty worthless because even the simplest things are hard for me!" My outlook about myself was so unhealthy and it would have been just as easy to look at the ice cream and laugh at myself for being absent-minded.

Everyone does silly things like this from time to time, yet I allowed every little mistake to mentally beat me down. I allowed the negative seeds planted in my heart to control my outlook and attitudes in every situation.

The Holy Spirit has taught me that I need to take on the mind of Christ in order to see myself as Christ sees me. I need to look at situations through the eyes of righteousness, not through my pain. I have learned who I am in Christ and who Christ is in me. The Bible has taught me that I am a new creation in Christ, a partaker of the divine nature of God and an heir of God and joint heir with Jesus. I am blessed with every spiritual blessing and I am more than a conqueror and triumphant in Christ. I am seated in heavenly places, free from every yoke of bondage, free from the bondage of fear and free from the law of sin and death. I am an ambassador for Christ.

Even more, I am strong in the Lord and the power of His might. I am protected by His angels and able to do whatever it is God has called me to do. I have the peace of God which surpasses all understanding. I have the authority over the enemy and enjoy God's unprecedented favor. I have been redeemed, washed, sanctified and I have a great future filled with prosperity and hope. I can speak to my mountains and they must move because I can do all things through Christ who strengthens me. I abide in Christ and He abides in me;

therefore, I overcome all things by the blood of the Lamb and the word of my testimony.

I have learned how to change my thought process by learning to think as Jesus thinks and how to feel as Jesus feels. Many think this is impossible, yet the Word of God tells us that it is possible.

This is My commandment, that you love one another just as I have loved you.
John 15:12 NASB

This commandment begins with loving yourself. I have had to learn how to control and change the way I think about myself. I've learned to have loving thoughts about myself and as I am patient and gentle with myself; I am also able to be patient and gentle with others.

God is love, and He commands us to love as He does so that when our actions are loving actions we are doing the will of God. In order to love — really love — we must surrender to the power of the Holy Spirit and allow Him to work in us and through us. This cannot happen unless we are willing to do things God's way. Actually doing things God's way does not involve just gaining knowledge about Him or going to church and moving through the ritualistic procedures of religion. It involves desiring to become like Him and truly becoming love.

But the goal of our instruction is love from a pure heart and a good conscience and a sincere faith.
1 Timothy 1:5 NASB

How in the world can we even think of becoming love if we can't even have thoughts of love? When someone does something to us, we can't seem to wait to get back at them. We sit and think thoughts of revenge. Come on now, you know I'm not the only one who has ever thought of ways to show someone else how it really is or should be.

We generally want to lash out of our own hurt instead of responding in compassion. We are selfish beings and are quick to see our pain, our hurt and our own way of thinking. Yet, when it comes to someone else we are so consumed with ourselves and what others have done to us that we can't see the other person's pain and hurt. Even if we see it, we believe our feelings are more important and our needs should come first.

The truth is, if someone is dishing out anything other than love, it is coming from some form of brokenness or insecurity within them. When Jesus looks at our actions, He interprets our intent. He knows the root cause of our words and responses.

> **For the word of God is living and active, and sharper than any two-edged sword, and piercing as far as the division of soul and spirit, of both joints and marrow, and able to judge the thoughts and intentions of the heart.**
> **Hebrews 4:12 NASB**

Rose-colored glasses of love find no fault, only mercy. We need to put on our rose-colored glasses so we can give grace to those who hurt us by choosing to see all the good and overlook the bad. Jesus sees all, yet He chooses to intercede for us, not condemn us. He chooses to forgive us, not judge us, and He chooses to walk in understanding with us even though He wouldn't do the same thing we just did.

Too often we judge others and choose to isolate ourselves from people because they don't do things our way. We also believe others are wrong because their thoughts and actions are different from our own. It is essential that we take on the mind of Christ and choose to think as the Word of God instructs. After all, is it not God who created every human being to think differently? It absolutely amazes me how God has created so many people and there are no two alike!

> **For My thoughts are not your thoughts, neither are your ways My ways, says the LORD. For as the heavens are higher than the earth, so are My ways higher than your ways, and My thoughts than your thoughts.**
> **Isaiah 55:8-9 KJV**

Now it is true that our thoughts are not His thoughts and we cannot know everything God thinks, but we can take on the mind of Christ by reading the Bible. We must make a conscious decision to gain knowledge of God and to change our thought processes accordingly.

For instance, as I learned that I am fearfully and wonderfully made in the eyes of God, I had a choice to continue to see myself as a worthless piece of junk or to start telling myself that I am wonderful in the eyes of my Creator.

> **I will praise thee; for I am fearfully and wonderfully made: marvelous are thy works; and that my soul knoweth right well.**
> **Psalm 139:14 KJV**

We choose the thoughts we meditate upon or daydream about. I spent most of my life thinking of how useless and unlovable I was instead of meditating on what my Creator sees in me.

I am not discounting the very painful circumstances we encounter along the way. I am saying that we can control the tendency to have them play over and over again in our head and heart. We can choose to daydream about what our Lord says about us and our situation and not what our surroundings tell us. Since I chose to begin thinking on the Word of God, my whole life has changed.

Yet, when we don't know who we are and who we were created to be, it is impossible to dwell on these good things. Therefore, knowledge of God's Word is essential in overcoming emotional and mental bondage. Knowing who you are in Christ is vital to having a healthy self-esteem.

The Holy Spirit is the perfect teacher, and when I opened my heart He was faithful to lead me to emotional freedom. I began realizing how the seeds of rejection infiltrated my thought processes.

For example, because I felt rejected by the people who were supposed to be the closest to me, my feelings led me to believe that nobody else wanted me either. I believed that although people were nice to me, they really didn't want me around simply for just who I was. I thought my presence was merely tolerated. My seeds of rejection were fueled by criticism. Growing up I was surrounded by people who believed criticism was a form of teasing. Whenever they joked, it was usually a way of putting me or someone else down. I allowed their ill manners to justify the way I felt about myself and life in general.

I have learned that I don't have to understand the source of the hurt in order to keep it from taking root in my life. I just have to remember that people who hurt others are hurting themselves.

When I look at all the criticism I have dealt with, I no longer allow it to condemn me or make me feel guilt and shame. I now understand that there is a difference between correction and criticism, and I realize that generally the person who is criticizing is dealing with their own insecurities. Now I pray for their deliverance.

All of us are guilty when it comes to dishing out our own baggage. I have learned that I can either walk away impaired and offended, or I can walk away choosing to forgive instantly even when I don't feel like forgiving. I can do this now because I know my emotions will line up with the decision I make. Forgiveness is the most powerful weapon available; it will heal and clean the soul. Forgiveness is a prerequisite of being emotionally and mentally free, and it isn't an option according to Christ.

For if you forgive men for their transgressions your heavenly Father will also forgive you. But if you do not forgive men, then your Father will not forgive your transgressions
Matthew 6:14-15 NASB

Until the end of our days we could keep on sharing all of our painful experiences and get absolutely nowhere. The only reason I have shared the hurts that I have experienced is to show that we must understand the root of our hurt and deal with it right from the source. Forgiveness involves the complete removal of the offense by confession and repentance. By forgiving, we are to dismiss and release everything associated with the violation.

We usually choose to remain in a state of blame because it is in our nature to do so. Just look at Adam and Eve: wasn't that the first thing they did? Adam blamed the woman and Eve blamed the serpent for their sin and disobedience. We can continue to blame, or we can be set free. It is our choice.

Not one of my family members is to blame for any of my problems. Even the words and actions of my step-mom is a reflection of her own pain from her childhood. She has many good qualities or my father would not have married her. She raised my three younger brothers in Christian schools and taught them from Scripture as they grew. The fruit of her labor shows itself in the remarkable men they have become. It just goes to show how we need to stand together helping each other through our own bondage, having compassion for one another and not creating division due to ignorant opinions and insensitive words. We are to bear one another's burdens.

> **Bear one another's burdens, and thus fulfill the law of Christ.**
> **Galatians 6:2 NASB**

I also recognize the generational curse of rejection and emotional bondage passed down on my mother's side of the family. Her father was an alcoholic and he emotionally abandoned her as a child. Going back many generations there is a history of brokenness in my family. I thank God that He has revealed the chain of destruction, and I must remind myself regularly that my battle is not against other people.

> **For we wrestle not against flesh and blood, but against principalities, against powers, against the rulers of the darkness of this world, against spiritual wickedness in high places.**
> **Ephesians 6:12 KJV**

I thank the Holy Spirit for teaching me how to recognize the root of negative seeds so I can dismiss them completely. When they try to creep up on me, I can choose to see them for what they really are - a weapon of the enemy.

I would like to challenge you to be honest with yourself and ask what types of seeds you plant on a regular basis. Make sure that when you look inwardly you not only see from the inside out, but also from the outside in. Take an inventory of the damage you have done with your ill-spoken words and choose never again to plant seeds for the enemy! Only plant seeds of love and compassion for one another. Your words are the most powerful tools you will ever be given. Use them wisely.

I pray that the Lord will reveal to you the deep-rooted seeds that have kept you from fulfilling your God-given destiny, and that He will show you how the truth of forgiveness will set you free just as it has for me.

CHAPTER FIVE

Your Beliefs Determine Your Path

*I*t took me two years to share my out-of-body experience with anyone because I didn't think anyone would believe me. For those two years I was horribly tormented by the enemy and I ran from my responsibility of believing the truth and trusting God completely. I did what was natural for me to do, and that was to satisfy my flesh. Longing for affection and intimacy, I did what most of us do: I went looking for my need to be met and indulged in sin.

My family and I started going to church at least three times a week and I began growing in the knowledge of God and His sovereignty. However, I was immature, confused and didn't believe it was my responsibility to be emotionally whole. I thought that God should just reach on the inside of me and instantly make me into what His Word said I should be and at the same time He should give me everything I wanted. I didn't want to take responsibility for my own soul. It was much easier to blame God for not changing me than to do it myself. Blaming God and others kept me from receiving restoration and it allowed me to justify my disobedience to God.

I selfishly started partying again, ran around trying to ignore the truth and I kept on wanting everything. I continued to solve my problems the only way I knew how. I was maintaining my unhealthy coping skills instead of falling on my face before God and standing for what I knew was right. I was weak and not ready to face any more heartache in my state of turmoil. In the process, I was creating an atmosphere around myself that was confusing even to me.

Here I was: I had just experienced the horrid eternal consequences of not serving Christ and yet I turned right back around and did many of the same things that I had done before I gave my life over to serve Jesus. Even though I now had love in my heart for Christ, I didn't understand this vicious cycle of destruction - the cycle of sin.

I trusted myself and counted on my boyfriend to fill my need for intimacy. Still, down deep I knew the only one to dissolve my loneliness was the Holy Spirit.

My indulgence in sin was no secret. After living this way for so long, I couldn't imagine how I could tell people that I had actually died and then been given a second chance to live? I feared people's opinion of me, and I knew that I needed to care more about what God thought of me than what people thought of me.

And they overcame him by the blood of the Lamb and by the word of their testimony; and they loved not their lives unto the death.
Revelation 12:11 KJV

I had to become honest with myself, realizing that everyone struggles with the desires of the flesh. Now that I was a new creature in Christ, it was time to discipline my desires and follow truth. I needed to put off the old man and not live after the vanity of the mind or the greediness of my own desires. I needed to follow after truth inwardly as well as outwardly. My selfish pursuit of filling my own needs instead of allowing the Heavenly Father to meet them caused this vicious cycle of heartache which can only be broken by a total surrender of your life and problems to the Lord Jesus Christ. I should not have depended on the world's coping skills to solve problems or just endure them. Rebelling against God is simply choosing to trust self instead of the supreme authority over your life.

Jesus wants the very best for us, and He doesn't want us living a miserable, tormented life. He wants us to have peace in the middle of our storms and rest under the covering of His wings, all the while knowing He is truly in control.

After my "out-of-body" experience I had become very sensitive to the spiritual world. The Bible refers to it as a gift of discernment – the ability to detect good from evil. I remember one particular night when I was laying in bed. Demons came into my room and manifested themselves. I recognized them as demons because they were beings without physical bodies and emanated intense fear. They attacked me by pinning me down to the bed and choking me! I was terrified and unable to scream.

I understood that these demons were trying to actually take my soul and damn me eternally before I was willing to tell the truth about my journey to Hell. I couldn't yell for help with my voice, but I cried out to God inwardly from my heart, "Jesus, help me!" He answered me by sending an angel. This angel walked into my room, took my hand and lowered his head as if to pray. Instantly all the evil spirits vanished out the window of my room.

Even in my disobedience, He sent an angel to my bedside. I knew at that very moment I could not keep my experience to myself any longer. I repented to the Father for my disobedience. From that moment on, any time an evil spirit would approach me I would just tell it, "In the name of Jesus and by the power of the blood of the cross, I command you to go!" Without fail the evil spirits would leave because they have to obey believers who understand the power in the name of Jesus.

I have had people tell me of their encounters with demonic spirits, and when would they tell them to leave, they won't go. You must believe! If you do not have faith and trust in the name of Jesus alone, your enemy will devour you. God has given you authority over all principalities and there is no power that compares to the resurrection power of Christ. Faith is the activating force in our life.

Our world is a spiritual world, and you must be aware that our enemy is real and is searching for whom he can destroy. Our enemy's purpose is to steal, kill and destroy. He wants to steal your life, your value, your self-worth, your joy, your strength and most importantly your personal walk with Jesus.

Many people wonder about the reality of the spiritual world, but I'm here to tell you that you no longer have to wonder. I have personally experienced many encounters with the enemy and I can reassure you that everything the Bible has to say is true. Just because it was written long ago doesn't mean that this world has changed spiritually.

My fear was realized when I went to tell my parents of my experience. They tried to be somewhat supportive, but they didn't understand. They were instead baffled. If I had really experienced Hell, then why did it take me so long to tell them and why had I decided to walk in disobedience? They didn't realize that my brokenness and spiritual immaturity had a lot to do with my disobedience to Christ. I really didn't understand that all it takes to allow God to meet your needs is to trust Him.

My pastor was the second person I told, and he appeared to understand me as well as my fears. He encouraged me and offered sound instruction and wisdom on what to do with my experience and how to overcome my fears. It took me many years to be able to share my testimony freely and without any fear of how others would receive it.

As I have grown in the Word of God, He has set me free from my fears. Although I knew that fear was the opposite of faith, I had to learn how to apply faith in my life and not fear.

Whatever beliefs or fears you embrace will be manifested in your life; this is a spiritual principle. If you believe that your fears will come to pass, then they will because that is where you are placing your faith. Your belief system determines not only your path in life, but your quality of life. We must also understand that beliefs are different from knowledge.

The belief system of so many people has become distorted. One reason is the fact that we have too many Christian groups to count these days, most of which allow Scripture to be manipulated to make it say and mean whatever conveniently fits a particular season in life. If all the denominations that profess Christianity really believed that Scripture is all about unconditional love, then we wouldn't have so many disagreements and divisions among Christians. A huge problem is that most people really don't even know what they believe.

I believe the greatest fear we face today is the fear of others and what they will think of us. We don't recognize or admit it because we are too busy justifying our actions and not realizing the consequences. We need to stop excusing our way out of sin. The only fear we should have is a reverent fear of God and this should be greater than any other need.

In the Garden of Eden, God gave Adam authority and dominion over everything in this world. Adam was to rule and reign over the earth and everything in it. Adam then lost his authority when he became disobedient and surrendered to Satan. He seduced Adam and Eve through their emotions, not their knowledge of the truth. Satan does that very same thing to all of us. He keeps us bound by emotion so that we won't walk in the authority we have been given.

Our emotions must be controlled by the thoughts that are found in the Word of God. When we can get our thought life and our emotions in line with God's Word, then success can come our way. When we have a failure mentality, we will think like a failure, feel like a failure and our actions will come from our thoughts and feelings. This means, of course, that we shall fail. We end up living out the results of our thoughts and feelings.

So many times in my life I have allowed myself to be seduced by my emotions and feelings stemming from pain or pleasures which have led me away from the will of God. God did not give us emotions so that we would be governed or controlled by them; He gave us emotions to bind us together in love.

Beloved, I wish above all things that you may prosper and be in health, even as thy soul prosper.
3 John 1:2 KJV

As we take back the control and authority over our lives by realizing the tools of our enemy, victory is ours. God desires to prosper and bless his children and He wants us to be a reflection of His wisdom, wealth, peace and joy. In order for us to prosper as God intended, we must stand up in faith by believing and claiming the promises of God which are to be fulfilled in our lives. We must choose to speak them over ourselves and our family everyday and also declare victory over every situation. We must make the decision to have our thoughts, emotions and actions line up with God's Word and then we will truly see His promises come to pass in our lives.

CHAPTER SIX

Eternal Consequences

O h, my precious, precious friend. Have you begun to grasp this amazing reality? Can you possibly comprehend the magnitude of this truth? The absolute truth of eternal damnation is real and does exist after you leave this earth.

Scripture so plainly tells us about our future, yet our own self-righteous attitudes block our comprehension and cause us to believe that judgment will never happen to us. The delusion is that God is too good to send us to Hell. We must realize that we cannot justify ourselves into Heaven. We send ourselves to hell even though it's against God's will.

The Word says that we must have no other Gods before Him. Just as parents set rules in place for their children, so our Heavenly Father gives us rules for our own benefit. Many of us say with our mouth that we love God more than anything else, yet our daily routine has nothing to do with Him. Just because we go to church and pray over our food doesn't mean we love God with all our heart. We must look inward to discover our actual motive for the things we do and our purpose for living every moment.

Excuses won't cut it when we stand face to face with our Creator. As sure as you were born, you will stand before the righteous Judge. It isn't about what you do *for* God — it's about *loving Him*.

> **Not everyone that says unto me, Lord, Lord, shall enter into the kingdom of heaven; but he that doeth the will of my Father which is in heaven. Many will say to me in that day, Lord, Lord, have we not prophesied in thy name? and in thy name have cast out devils? and in thy name done many wonderful works? And then will I profess unto them, I never knew you: depart from me, ye that work iniquity.**
> **Matthew 7:21-23 KJV**

It's not about the work we do *for* Him, but it is about our motives behind our actions. At work we do many projects or tasks for our boss, but that doesn't necessarily mean we have to like him or her. In actuality, it means we are doing what is essential to achieve a desired result.

How many of us live our lives by doing "things" for personal gain? For example, many of us working together can give millions and millions of dollars to the poor. Do you think all the money is given out of a desire to be obedient to God in order to take care of the widows and fatherless? Does giving make us feel better simply by knowing that we've done our part?

No matter why we give, it is good to give. However, the only giving that matters is the giving you do for Christ himself. All of us have different motives for the things we do — what is your motive? Are you brave enough to answer yourself honestly? A day is coming when you will stand under the microscope to have your real motives revealed. Thank God for His grace which He gives freely to all of us. We simply have to ask.

By faith we receive and by God's binding love we are able to have a relationship with our Lord Jesus Christ. Our actions reflect our relationships as well as who we are individually. When we have a close relationship with Jesus, it shows through the way we live just as it does in a good marriage. When you and your spouse take on one another's character traits, you begin to blend together as one. When Jesus is a part of your life, the Light of God shines through for all to see.

When I experienced Hell there was utter darkness, a pure darkness where light was completely absent. The reason it was so dark was because Jesus was not present there. Jesus is the Light.

Jesus spoke to them saying, "I am the light of the world; he who follows Me shall not walk in darkness, but shall have the light of life."
John 8:12 NASB

I now have complete understanding of His declaration, "I am the light of the world." In Hell, the place where I was, Jesus was nowhere to be found. Therefore, there was no light at all, only pure and ultimate darkness. Life equals light and death equals darkness.

The first thing God did was to create the light and separate the light from the darkness. This light that is referred to in Genesis is the redemption plan for man. Jesus Christ is the Light and He is our redemption. It is because of the blood sacrifice of the Lamb that was slain that you and I can enter into this Light.

God himself is all knowing and before the foundations of the earth He knew the struggles you would face. He knew all men would sin and fall short of the victory, so Adam and Eve's disobedience was not a surprise. God's love for us is so great, the very first thing He did was develop a plan to maintain a relationship with us. He prepared a way for our salvation.

> **In the beginning God created the heavens and the earth. And the earth was without form, and void; and darkness was upon the face of the deep. And the Spirit of God moved upon the face of the waters. And God said, Let there be light and there was light. And God saw the light, that it was good; and God divided the light from the darkness.**
> **Genesis 1:1-4 KJV**

It is clear that this Light is different from the light by which we see physical things because it wasn't until the fourth day that the sun and moon were created.

> **And God said, Let there be lights in the firmament of the heaven to divide the day from the night; and let them be for signs, and for seasons, and for days and years; And let them be for lights in the firmament of the heaven to give light on the earth; and it was so. And God made two great lights: the greater light to rule the day, and the lesser light to rule the night; He made the stars also and God set them in the firmament of the heaven to give light upon the earth, And to rule over the day and over the night, and to divide the light from the darkness; and God saw that it was good and the evening and the morning were the fourth day.**
> **Genesis 1:14-19 KJV**

This gives a deeper meaning to day and night. The light of each day reflects the glory and guidance of our God, but the night reflects sin. Think about it: when you are a child of the Light (Jesus), meaning you are a true believer, your activities are centered around that light and good things happen. However, when you are a child of the night, meaning you aren't a true follower of Christ or you are living in bondage, then your activities are centered around darkness and no good comes from them.

For example, when do people engage in "partying?" or when is most crime committed? Nighttime is when most inappropriate behavior plays into so called "fun" for a person who isn't obeying God's Word. I can't think of one good thing that comes from living that type of lifestyle. Pain, heartache and bondage comes from living in sin and darkness.

Now, I am not saying that once the sun sets and it becomes dark that nothing good is taking place. There are many great things that happen at night, yet I am focusing on the lifestyle choices we make. Are we choosing to be children of light or children of darkness?

For you were formerly darkness, but now you are light in the Lord; walk as children of light.
Ephesians 5:8 NASB

I am absolutely astonished at the fact that God allowed me to see all three heavens and the separation that is between them. Oh, how I wish I could paint the perfect picture to show you the specific detail of the division.

And God said, Let there be a firmament in the midst of the waters, and let it divide the waters from the waters. And God made the firmament, and divided the waters which were under the firmament from the waters which were above the firmament; and it was so. And God called the firmament Heaven. And the evening and the morning were the second day.
Genesis 1:6-8 KJV

Just as Genesis describes, there are three distinct places: the universe (including our solar system), Heaven, where God the Father dwells and Hell, where the enemies of the one true God are sent. I was able to see all three and I was also able to look out beyond the place of damnation and look upon the entire creation as well as the separation of these three specific areas of existence. I was not bound by the normal limitations of our physical eyes.

Our universe is shaped like an elongated disc with very specific parameters. Each "firmament" has a stopping and starting point and is divided by a large space of nothingness. It is absolutely amazing!

To live means to be in the presence of the Lord and to die means to be separated from God's presence. There is a physical death which is the separation of the soul from the body, and then there is a second death which is an eternal separation of the unbeliever from God in the lake of fire.

But for the cowardly, and unbelieving, and abominable, and murderers, and immoral, and sorcerers, and idolaters, and all liars, their part will be in the lake that burns with fire and brimstone, which is the second death.
Revelation 21:8 NASB

My friend, know there are eternal consequences to every decision you make! I pray you are making the right decision: the decision to live covered by the blood of Jesus.

This is the very reason Jesus died on the cross. His love for us is so great that He doesn't want us to be banished from Him forever. He desires a relationship with each and every one of us, yet we often turn away from our relationship with Him because it is easy to blame Him for our problems and run from the truth. Our enemy encourages us to focus on our problems and inadequacies instead of on the hope and love of God.

It is our enemy's goal to separate us from God and he is always lurking over our shoulder to condemn us for the mistakes we make. If we could only realize the mercy and grace that God gives to us no matter how many times we mess up.

For God so loved the world that He gave His only begotten Son, that whosoever believes in him should not perish but have everlasting life
John 3:16 KJV

I know that for some of you it is difficult to believe what I am saying. You may be thinking that if you completely accept what I say as the truth, then this would require change on your part and you're not ready to make any changes. Possibly it's just hard to accept that there are consequences to our sin? God tells us how to escape destruction, but most of us are just too stubborn to listen.

Jesus said unto him, I am the way, the truth, and the life; No man comes unto the Father but by me."
John 14:6 KJV

If I have told you earthly things and you believe not, how will you believe, if I tell you of heavenly things?
John 3:12 KJV

We can't even come close to understanding what lies ahead for us in eternity. God didn't design this life for us to understand things ahead. His design for us is to understand that life is all about Him. Heaven and Hell are real, and the things you choose to seek after will determine where you go and what you will become.

I wasn't in Hell just because of my attempted suicide; I was there because Jesus was not Lord of my life. The way you die is not important but it's the condition that your soul is in when you die that matters. Granted, if I had known Jesus before this happened, I wouldn't have even considered suicide.

I know there have been many people who have committed suicide and claimed to know Jesus. I can't speak for them or where they are for eternity — only God knows and He is a just judge. Yet, I do know there is a difference between just knowing Jesus exists and is real versus really taking the extra step to make Him Lord over their lives.

Please, I beg you to listen to this warning! Hell is real and I experienced it. Every second you delay in bowing down before Almighty God is one you can't afford to waste. You aren't guaranteed another second in this life because God owes you nothing, yet you owe Him everything. Jesus paid a debt He did not owe and we owe a debt we cannot pay.

> **... that at the name of Jesus every knee should bow, of those who are in heaven, and on earth, and under the earth.**
> **Philippians 2:10 NASB**

Every knee will bow and every tongue will confess Jesus as Lord. The question is this: Will you do it now and live your life serving Him, or will you be stubborn believing you know what's best for your own life and have plenty of time to do it later? If "later" is in your heart, then you might end up confessing with great sorrow. If "later" never comes, then there won't be any way for you to turn back and change the eternal decision you have made once this life is over. Self-righteousness will destroy your soul, so I urge you to search your heart, repent of your sins and confess Jesus as Lord now. Live your life for Him or you will end up where I was experiencing torment that knows no end.

When you hear the word hell, you think of the kind of heat you feel when you burn your finger. That couldn't be further from the truth. A burn is actually a loving gentle touch compared to the sensation I felt in that dreadful place of torment. I would describe it as much more than a feeling because you actually become sin. You turn into a being of death. I learned that the real meaning of death is to be absent from God. The Word of God tells us that God is love and to be absent from that love is to be in the presence of everything that love is not - death.

God is love. He doesn't just *have* love, He *is* love and only good (love) comes from Him. For example, it is utterly impossible for Him to tell a lie. Therefore, if you turn into love you can't tell a lie, you can only tell the whole truth. You won't be able to do anything but pure righteous acts of goodness.

Just the opposite happens when you turn into fear - all you do is sin. It is easy to lie, manipulate, be deceitful and act out of selfishness because that is what you are and righteousness is not in you. A spider is not a flower. It doesn't look like a flower and it doesn't smell like a flower because you can't be something you're not.

Sin is progressive in our hearts. Once you commit adultery or any other sin, it gets easier each time you give in to it. Whatever you feed your mind and heart is eventually what you will become. We must be careful of the "soul food" we take in. For instance, most Americans are so intrigued by the entertainment world that it influences how we dress, the things we buy, the reputation we want to have and how we live our lives. This is truly a deceptive tool of our enemy. God wants His people to be blessed, but not in the way Hollywood portrays it. Our society's standards are completely contrary to God's Word, yet we spend the majority of our time feasting on entertainment by filling our minds and hearts with lies and deception.

This life is just the beginning and the way we live it will determine everything in our eternal future. Yet, because eternity is such a large subject and one that we tend to steer away from, its relevance in our thought life fades quickly. Oh, if we could just get a speck of comprehension of the purpose of our being.

The way you choose to live your life will determine whether or not you turn into sin or become love for eternity. Jesus is the only One and true God. In His Word He tells us that His children will be changed.

> **In a moment, in the twinkling of an eye, at the last trump:. for the trumpet shall sound, and the dead shall be raised incorruptible, and we shall be changed.**
> **1 Corinthians 15:52 KJV**

Reading this verse causes us to wonder, *What will we be changed into?* Most people think of just the new body we will receive and consider this as the change. There is far more to it than that.

> **And God said, Let us make man in Our image, after to Our likeness.**
> **Genesis 1:26 KJV**

In Scripture God is represented in three parts: God the Father, God the Son and God the Holy Spirit. Man is also in three parts: body, soul and spirit. A man's soul is in three parts: mind, emotions and will. I believe that when we are changed and given our new eternal bodies, we will remain in three parts but will be transformed into a being of love. God is love and our enemy is everything love is not. Our enemy is real and is doing everything possible to deceive us and keep us from seeking to know Jesus Christ with all that we are and all that we could ever possibly become.

I was not seeking to become like Christ in my former lifestyle; I was seeking to have my every need met. In my pursuit for freedom I found bondage which nearly destroyed my soul. The enemy deceived me and I became as my enemy, cast out from a loving God forever. I am so grateful for the love and mercy He has shown me.

God tells us in His Word that He is transforming His children. His work for us is to become love so pure, so real, so magnificent that it is beyond this world or anything in it. Love is what we all desire to become — we just don't realize it. We have a choice in life to become pure love or horrid sin. What has your choice been so far?

He who began a good work in you will perfect it until the day of Christ Jesus.
Philippians 1:6 NASB

CHAPTER SEVEN

Hope for the Future

Gratefulness overwhelms me when I think of how fortunate I am to be alive today. It was certainly not by my choice, but it was by God's divine design for my life. How could God show one person so much mercy and love when it was so undeserved? I have committed almost every sin I think there is to commit. I have placed myself and my needs before my service to God, therefore putting myself above God. I have done some pretty ruthless things and in no way do I deserve any kindness from above — actually, none of us do, no not one!

It doesn't matter if you've lived your life having obeyed all the rules, because it is not your works that get you into heaven. Eternal life with God only comes through the saving grace of the blood of Jesus Christ which was shed on Calvary. You don't get close to God by earning a relationship based on works. The blessing of intimacy with God is received through faith.

The only reason I am here today is because God is faithful and is true to His word. He tells us that if anyone should call upon the name of the Lord, they will be saved. That is what I did; I called on the name of Jesus to forgive me and He was faithful.

And it shall come to pass, that whosoever shall call on the name of the Lord shall be saved.
Acts 2:21 KJV

All of us are sinners who can't even begin to comprehend the love of God. We just know that He loved us so much that He sent His only Son to be the perfect blood sacrifice for our sins. Jesus was God manifested in the flesh, the Word made flesh and He willingly died for us so that we don't have to be separated from Him.

When Jesus was hanging on the cross in complete agony, totally innocent of any wrong doing, He did nothing but cry out for us saying:

Father, forgive them; for they know not what they do.
Luke 23:34 KJV

We may not understand the impact of our sin, but we must comprehend that we have been forgiven if we just simply ask. It doesn't matter how bad the crime was that you committed or how unwanted or unworthy you feel. God wants to wash you clean with His saving blood and He wants to have a close relationship with you throughout eternity.

In the very beginning, God himself walked in the Garden of Eden every day and Adam and Eve communed with Him. God simply wanted to talk to Adam and have a relationship with him. God hasn't changed the purpose of our creation and we are to bring Him glory by drawing close to Him.

God understands and knows that we have nothing to offer Him but junk. Issues and problems are everywhere you turn, and at times it is very difficult to see through the garbage and maintain a positive outlook. However, God sees our problems as opportunities for Him to be our Provider, our Healer, our Peace, our Strength, our Joy, our Savior and our Answer. He wants us to cry out to Him so He can take all our pain away. He can show us the way to victory and the precious Holy Spirit can guide us into perfect harmony.

I have grown to know and love Jesus as my best friend. I talk to Him just as I would talk to you. Whether I am working, running errands, sitting at home or driving down the road He is right there beside me. The spirit of the Lord is in the atmosphere. I work at cultivating and growing my relationship with my Lord.

Once you have humbly asked Jesus to be the Lord of your life and cleanse you from all unrighteousness, then you are in the position to actually experience the presence of God for yourself just as the priests did in the Old Testament. In the Old Testament, the presence of God dwelled in the Holy of Holies in the Temple, but when Jesus Christ died on the cross, the outermost veil of the temple was ripped and now every person can enter into the Holy Place to draw near to the Almighty.

> **Know ye not that ye are the temple of God, and that the Spirit of God dwelleth in you?**
> **1 Corinthians 3:16 KJV**
>
> **Know ye not that your body is the temple of the Holy Ghost which is in you!**
> **1 Corinthians 6:19 KJV**

The moment you repent and confess Jesus as your Lord, the Spirit of God comes to live and dwell on the inside of you. This is possible because you are two-thirds spirit and one-third flesh.

I have learned to come unto the Lord offering Him thanksgiving for all things, even though sometimes I don't feel thankful. I have had to learn to humbly praise Him for who He is and to commune with Him as Adam did: talking to Him, listening to Him and worshipping Him. As a result, I am now experiencing the true joy of life.

Now faith is the substance of things hoped for, the evidence of things not seen.
Hebrews 11:1 KJV

I had to learn how to receive the Word of God into my life by faith. The Word of God is the healing power that is willing and able to set us free from all our pain and sorrow. The Word is sharp and piercing, and it can divide and conquer all things if we will just let it do its work within us. It has divided and conquered all my problems, for God has always been at work in my life. His mercy is continually pouring out over me and I experience His righteous acts of goodness regularly. The God I serve is just sitting there waiting for us to call upon His name so that He may save us from our bondage and from a life of misery. He doesn't desire for us to live miserable, unhappy lives.

He desires for us to rejoice daily and enjoy the simplicities of life itself. We should be showing our appreciation for the smell of fresh cut flowers on a spring morning, a little hummingbird flying around your yard, the children laughing and playing and the soft breeze that keeps you cool on a warm day. He is trying to show us His love and mercy all around, and I encourage you to stop whatever it is you do and enjoy the simple creation He has put before you. When you look around, see the beauty; see the positive and not the negative driving force which keeps our heads slumped over in despair.

Road rage is becoming more prevalent because we are a society so full of pain, anger and unforgiveness. We justify our actions by our opinion or viewpoint and it only leads to misery. Antidepressants are one of the most popular drugs sold today. We are living in a depressed state and teaching our children rebellion and promiscuity as a way of life. At what point do we say that enough is enough and admit that we are ready to change and make a difference in our own life as well as in the lives of others?

You will influence everyone you come in contact with to one degree or another. We influence one another simply by being ourselves. Are we going to continue teaching self-destruction as a way of escape?

Self-discipline seems to have become a dirty word today, yet it is the very thing that will allow you to enter into the presence of God. You will be able to offer up to Him a living sacrifice, a sacrifice that is worthy and acceptable to Him.

I don't know about you, but I want to be a godly influence whether I'm sitting in the car, walking down the street or simply by choosing what I should watch on TV. I want the people I come into contact with to recognize the love and mercy of God in my life. One of the first things people notice is attitude because attitudes portray your thought life.

We must learn to discipline our thought life by dismissing every thought that doesn't line up with God's Word and then refusing to dwell on it.

Casting down imaginations, and every high thing that exalteth itself against the knowledge of God, and bringing into captivity every thought to the obedience of Christ.
2 Corinthians 10:5 KJV

As children of God, we must learn how to train our thoughts and mind to focus on things that are good.

> **Finally, brethren, whatsoever things are true, whatsoever things are honest, whatsoever things are just, whatsoever things are pure, whatsoever things are lovely, whatsoever things are of good report; if there be any virtue, and if there be any praise, think on these things.**
>
> **Philippians 4:8 KJV**

It is difficult not to fall in the wide trap of "society conditioning." For example, our society wants us to believe that a woman's beauty comes from being a sex symbol, but the Word tells us that a godly woman is the true desire of a man. Shallow surface thinking is normally a sign of deception, and true purity comes with a high price that few are willing to pay. My heart's desire is to stand pure in the eyes of God, not the eyes of the world.

All the answers we have ever searched for are right in front of our face. We only need to open our eyes and search for truth because God is no respecter of persons. He is willing to touch any and all who call upon His Name and hope is found in the saving arms of Jesus Christ. His presence is a place to find rest and restitution and a place where total serenity is found and kept. Humility will take you to the feet of Jesus and His love will keep you there.

His love keeps me focused on the things above, not below and He teaches me to think on things which are to come and to daydream about heavenly things, not earthly things. He teaches me that we are beings of priority in the spiritual realm; after all, He says we are higher than the angels.

We will rule and reign with Him throughout eternity! We are a priesthood, a holy nation made up of all true believers from all over the world. As the children of God, we are to offer up praises towards our Savior who has called us out of darkness and into His marvelous light. If just one person praying can put one thousand angels into flight, doesn't that tell you that we hold a special position in the eyes of God?

We have a future filled with promise and we will be engulfed with glory unspeakable and full of pure joy. We learn to rest in the arms of the King of Kings by simply falling down before Him and pouring out our hearts. We underestimate God's desire to meet our needs according to His plan and not the crooked ones we set for ourselves.

> **For I know the plans that I have for you, declares the LORD, plans for welfare and not for calamity, to give you a future and a hope.**
> **Jeremiah 29:11 NASB**

CHAPTER EIGHT

Abide in Christ

My heart's desire is to share with you the love and power of the almighty, magnificent God. His love is perfect and it conquers all things. So often, many of us think we are unworthy of His love and so undeserving of receiving His forgiveness. Then we believe that God is too far away to touch us. We may feel we are just one small speck in a great big world and that our cares are not worth His time. We wonder why we have gone through such suffering if God really does love us.

> **The Spirit of the Lord God is upon me; because the LORD hath anointed me to preach good tidings unto the meek; he hath sent me to bind up the brokenhearted, to proclaim liberty to the captives, and the opening of the prison to them that are bound; To proclaim the acceptable year of the LORD, and the day of vengeance of our God; to comfort all that mourn; To appoint unto them that mourn in Zion, to give unto them beauty for ashes, the oil of joy for mourning, the garment of**

praise for the spirit of heaviness; that they might be called trees of righteousness, the planting of the LORD, that he might be glorified.
Isaiah 61:1-3 KJV

I do not have all the answers to our suffering, but what I do know is that the enemy is the one who initiated disobedience in the Garden of Eden. As a result, pain and suffering have been a part of life in this world, often in horrific ways. The foundation of suffering is sin and disobedience, but oh what a Savior we have! Our Savior is patiently waiting for you to come to Him and open your heart and ask Him for restoration. Only Jesus Christ can restore your broken heart.

The thief comes only to steal and kill and destroy; I came that they may have life, and have it abundantly.
John 10:10 NASB

The Holy Spirit was faithful to provide the revelation that broke me free from the oppression I had suffered for years. One day a small, still voice deep inside of me, the Holy Spirit, ever so gently asked me, "Are you my servant?" I quickly responded, "Yes." Then the Holy Spirit asked, "Why are you trying to have two masters when you know you can only have one?" With confusion, I asked for Him to explain my heart and the reasoning behind His question.

I saw a flash-back of the past several years of my life and realized how I consistently fell down in a certain area. I would walk in obedience as carefully as I could, always calling on God to help me fill the void in my life. Then I would wonder why the void still remained. I would continue to veer off the path little by little until I tumbled down to a crash. When I found myself in more turmoil than I could handle, I would repent. I'd live for God awhile again, and then before I knew it I would find myself turning just a little to the left to get my void filled. The cycle would repeat itself over and over.

I responded by saying to God, "I see the cycle I'm caught up in, and I have cried out for years for You to remove it, yet You refuse. I don't want to be in this vicious cycle anymore! Why have You chosen not to take this from me? Why have You chosen to allow me to continue in my suffering? All I need is one touch to be whole and You have withheld Your hand."

Feeling self-pity, anger and brokenness, I couldn't understand why I could try so hard and yet still fall short. I spent years asking to be repaired and never received the "fix." Thankfully, the Holy Spirit was faithful. He gave me the answer that was long awaited when my heart was finally ready to receive that answer.

The Lord revealed that He had been waiting on me to surrender my disobedience to him and give Him my whole heart, not just a few layers. He was waiting for me to make the decision to be obedient even if my needs went unmet.

He revealed that in certain areas of my life I was only serving Him to fill a need. When He didn't perform the way I thought He should, I would find a way to meet my own desires. I was serving myself instead of Him.

The Lord showed me that I must serve Him in complete obedience without judging if He met my needs and desires according to my own thoughts. I had to learn that in order for Him to fulfill my desires, His work in me had to be allowed to go deep into the recesses of my heart. More often than not, there is more work to be done inside of my spirit than I realize. I must be willing to be a true servant no matter what it costs, and disobedience is never the solution.

With an outpouring of tears and with my whole heart, I repented and committed to put Him first. I made the choice never to seek after my needs again. I really meant it from all that was in me. Amazingly enough, within twenty-four hours the void within me was filled and never again have I felt that horrible emptiness.

Making the decision to be obedient, even if my emotional desires and needs were never met again, was not an easy decision to make. I had to learn to trust and have complete faith that the Holy Spirit will take care of me regardless of my circumstances, situations or relationships.

God wants to abide in our lives. He wants His presence to engulf us daily, yet we push Him away by our unwillingness to put Him first. We freely say with our mouth that He is lord of our lives, but deep within our hearts we are really placing trust in ourselves before relying solely on God. We can't trust ourselves more than we trust God.

Abiding in Christ means to remain beside Him in perseverance. We are to continue in the relationship no matter what happens, endure and trust in the relationship with persistent loyalty, cleave to Him without letting go and staying put with focus and purpose.

My focus was all about my void, my lack and my Heavenly Father revealed to me that my relationship with Him had been more one-sided than anything else. I was willing to do what He asked if it was convenient. I would reach out and minister His Word to others if the conditions were right, but my main priority was to meet my own needs – not His.

How would a good friend of yours feel if all you did was ask for money to pay off your debt? What if you just expected them to solve the problems of your family members so you could get along with them? Maybe all you ever do is talk about your needs and yet you never met any of your friend's needs because you're so consumed with yourself. This poor friend would more than likely feel that the relationship was all about you and finally come to realize that you are using them for all you can get.

Relationships are a two-way street, and God desires to have a relationship with us because we are His children - His creation. Although God has absolutely no lack, He needs His people to worship Him and He requires us to be an extension of His love. Our heart should be open to giving compassion to those around us, to show mercy to the hurting and to be His hands and His feet. Our priorities should be to speak and show Him to the world and spend every moment of every day seeking to fill the needs of others.

If we do not want to suffer "lack", then we need to make it our first priority to worship God by meeting the needs of those around us. As we lay down our own needs, we trust the Holy Spirit to make perfect provision for our soul to be healthy and joyful. When we put Him first, God will pour out blessings we cannot contain! This only happens when our priorities are in the right place. He is a giving God and He wants His children to have it all.

Jesus is no respecter of persons and what He does for one He will do for another. He went to the cross for each one of us individually. The purpose for His death on the cross was to bring us life! This life is not only for eternity, but it applies to life right here on earth as well. This is the only way we will find a pain-free life full of laughter and joy and no more emotional roller coaster rides, no more vicious cycles of addiction and no more bitterness and hurt. Only He can give us a heart filled with peace that surpasses all understanding - a peaceful, submissive heart that is willing to humble itself and admit there is no other God before Him.

If God would stretch down His hand literally to the ends of the earth to save a person like me, then He will definitely do it for you as well. All I did was simply ask for Him to forgive me, and not only did He forgive me but He has spent every moment of my life teaching me my worth and value. He's been teaching me about Him and about the very purpose for which I was created. Every moment He's showing me how to walk in victory. He has poured out blessings upon my life in such a way that I never thought possible, and He is always making a way of escape for me. He's enabling and equipping me for each challenge I have to overcome. He has never left my side or turned His head and He is focused on me by always seeing every tear I shed, counting every bump and bruise and never letting me down because He is faithful and His love is unconditional.

God has placed so much value on his children: He has given them the power and authority over all things here on this earth, He has made a way for us to rule and reign with Him throughout eternity and He even sends His angels who are ministering spirits to bring comfort and deliverance.

Understanding our authority in Christ is important when desiring liberty. Jesus died on the cross not only to keep our souls with Him eternally, but He died so that death and destruction would be separated from our soul as we live life on this earth.

The earth was perfect and man was perfect in God's image before sin and disobedience came to be. Adam and Eve had never experienced sadness, loneliness, rejection, fear, or any other negative emotion or thought. Living in the Garden was like living in Heaven - there was no unrighteousness until Adam chose disobedience. When Christ went to the cross, He defeated the effects sin held over us. If we do not take our authority back we will suffer. Taking back what rightfully belongs to you, taking back the state your soul was designed for is simply a matter of understanding exactly what it is you have authority over. Although man is now in a sinful state and will not be completely delivered from that state until we leave this earth, we have the inherent right to take authority over the curse of sin in our lives.

We do this by telling sin to get out of our lives! For example if you suffer from fear you would say, "Fear, I command you in the name of Jesus and by the power of the resurrection to leave my mind, my emotions and my will. Separate yourself from my flesh because the blood of Jesus has cleansed me from all unrighteousness and you have no place in my life. I bind fear and loose the love of God throughout my soul to penetrate me and cause me to live in liberty of the truth. Thank you, Jesus, for the promise of your blessings to chase me down and consume my life."

Walking in the spirit is allowing the Holy Spirit permission to transform you back into the image of love and separate every characteristic trait that comes from the enemy. We must make a conscious decision to be obedient, bind sin and loose the love of God into our soul. Fighting with the weapons of our words and igniting faith in our soul is a choice we make.

You have value, and your worth is more prized than anything this earth has to offer. A relationship with the heavenly Father is worth more than gold, it is more valuable than silver and it is more precious and delicate than any beautiful jewel. He truly gives us His beauty for our ashes. He wants to trade our heartache for wholeness, our addictions for freedom, our pain for joy and our sickness for health. He wants us to be whole and free.

Love is freedom. If you can't forgive and love yourself and others, then you aren't free. Give your bondage to Jesus so that He can set you free.

So many people wonder how you talk to God. How do you give Him your inner burdens and allow Him to move in your life? It is so simple - you humble yourself before Him and acknowledge that He is God and that there is no one higher. Ask Jesus to be the Lord and Savior of your life and allow Him to wash you with the blood of Calvary. Thank Him for who He is and for the fact that He has revealed His sovereignty to you. Tell Him that you have nothing to offer Him but your burdens, and that you have nothing to give Him but pain and suffering, but you lay it all down at His feet. Let Him know you surrender all. There isn't anything more pleasing to the Father than for His child to come to Him for help and restitution.

Be still and know that He is Lord, and then trust Him for the answer. This will be the time for you to dry your tears and begin rejoicing through faith because you will know that His perfect love has washed away all your cares and made you brand new.

The Word tells us that we are to enter His gates with thanksgiving in our hearts and enter His courts with praise. Although you may not feel like it, do it by faith and with an obedient heart. Rest assured, you will enter the presence of the Almighty and will be transparent with all that is within you. You'll give Him the good, the bad and the ugly and know that you will never be the same. You will come out changed, renewed and redeemed.

God wants to take every broken piece of your life and use it for good. He wants to bind up your wounds and heal every bruise. God's Word is the medicine we need for our mind, our will and our emotions.

> **My son, give attention to my words; incline your ear to my sayings. Do not let them depart from your eyes; keep them in the midst of your heart; for they are life to those who find them, and health to all their flesh.**
>
> **Proverbs 4:20-22**

True freedom comes from abiding in God and God abiding in you. Meditating on Scripture, memorizing it and applying it to your life each and every day is the key to victory. We must continually make the decision to apply God's Word to our life and thoughts.

Too often we go to God on the basis of getting our needs met and not to surrender to His Lordship. Know that by becoming a servant we will become conquerors. As you take a stand to meet the needs of others and sacrifice your wants in order to serve Christ, there isn't anything good that will be withheld from you. God is a jealous God, and He wants to be more important than your need.

CHAPTER NINE

Jesus Is Our High Priest

The reason we are able to abide in the presence of the Almighty and the very reason we have the ability to come boldly before His throne to pursue a personal relationship with God is because Jesus Christ is our High Priest.

The Old Testament explains how the tabernacle was a sanctuary built according to the pattern of God's throne in heaven. This tabernacle was where God's presence had chosen to dwell with His people. In the outer courts, the people were allowed to enter for a time of thanksgiving and praise, and then there was an area where only the priesthood was allowed. Following strict instructions, the priesthood would make daily sacrifices so they could continually maintain the ordinances of God. Yet, behind the veil of the Holy of Holies was the actual presence of God. Once a year on the Day of Atonement, (Yom Kippur), the High Priest would enter into the Holy of Holies to offer a blood sacrifice for the sins of the people for the entire year. In God's presence he would make intercession for them and ask for mercy and grace.

The blood which was sprinkled on the Ark of the Covenant came from a bull and a goat which had to be perfect without spot or blemish. The High Priest even had to wear specific clothing because entering into the Holy of Holies was not something to be taken lightly. It was truly a matter of life or death, because if any mistake was made the priest would be killed by the power of God.

Jesus came as our High Priest and perfect sacrifice once and for all, and now He sits at the right hand of the Father continually making intercession for you and me. Through faith in Him, all of our sins can be forgiven if we truly repent and follow His instructions for living. We should choose to see Him for who He is and receive the truth, knowing that when He died on the cross the veil to the outer room of the Temple, or The Holy Place, was ripped so that all can now enter into the place where only the priests were originally allowed to worship. No longer do we go to another man for confession or for the need to intercede for us; we can go straight to the feet of Jesus to plead His blood upon our life, confessing the wrongs we have committed in full repentance and knowing He has the keys to life and destruction. We must understand that no one is turned away at His feet.

In our society we think of going to church as nothing more than a traditional religious act, completely overlooking the true meaning.

Learning about God and entering into His presence through means of praise and worship is truly the most important thing you will ever do in this life, and it should be taken seriously because it is a matter of eternal life or death for you and me.

Too many people focus on the problems in the lives of the people going to the church and use that for an excuse not to go or believe. I want to encourage you to turn your eyes on God, not the people, because focusing on others will keep you from God's best and possibly even from eternal life. Hypocrisy is a problem both in and out of the church because people don't always follow through with what they know is right. Each of us is responsible for our own personal relationship with God and without it you will only suffer.

Realize that God is omnipresent and knows our every thought and feeling. Know that nothing can be hidden from His sight. So, why do we continue to pretend that He doesn't see us as we run from Him? Why do we go on living our lives as we choose, not as He desires, and choose pride over humility? Let us confess our self-righteousness and unbelief and ask for faith, even if it's only the size of a mustard seed.

The Holy Spirit truly exists and wants to transform your life into something beautiful. He can take your sorrow, your ashes, and your painful experiences and turn them into something more beautiful than you ever imagined! All you have to do is believe!

If we would humbly ask the Lord to change our desires into His desires and stop living our life to meet our selfish cravings, we would see victory here in this life and in the life to come. God doesn't just want to set us free only for eternity; rather, He wants us to live free on this earth as well as in the world to come. To be free is to love and serve unconditionally, and if we aren't able to love everyone unconditionally without judgment or prejudice, then we aren't free. Love always hopes and love never puts self first.

There is a price for freedom, but this price has already been paid by Jesus. All He asks from us in return is a life of obedience to the commands or instructions of God and to surrender all to Him. By doing so, we can show our love for Him! If we would realize that as long as we are pursuing our own careers, our own relationships or our own way, we will never be satisfied. God designed a perfect life for us, one filled with opportunity and victory in our jobs as well as with family and friends. We simply need to let Him have the control He wants and deserves.

Where there is "lack" in your life, I will be bold enough to say it is because you lack intimacy with the Father in that area of your life. No priest nor pastor, bishop or any other religious office can take the place of a personal relationship with Jesus. We must take off the religious blinders and realize it isn't about structure or traditions, but rather it is about the cross and only the cross.

If we are looking for satisfaction in drugs, alcohol, sex, food, our work or any other thing, we are living a lie and are in rebellion toward God. The thinking goes that we know what is best for our own life and we will deal with God when the time is right.

The purpose of the cross is now clear to me. The reason Jesus suffered and died is so we don't have to suffer through our problems. We can rise above them through His grace and power, and we don't have to be separated from the presence of God in this life or the life to come. It is the cleansing blood of Christ that washes us whiter than snow, removing every spot and blemish and healing every bump and bruise. God truly desires to commune with you.

It is our reasonable service to present our bodies as a living sacrifice, holy and acceptable unto to God. Are we not the tabernacle in which God himself has chosen to dwell? When Jesus died and the veil was ripped, from that moment forward God chose to place His presence in the hearts of those who would welcome Him into their lives.

From the fruit of our lips we should continually offer up thanksgiving and praise for what He has done and is going to do. We now have a High Priest who is able to touch our infirmity, a High Priest who was tempted in all things yet remained perfect. He understands us better than we understand ourselves, and He is waiting for us to humble ourselves before Him.

Those who dwell in the secret place of the most High shall abide in the shadows of the almighty. God is our fortress and our deliverer. As we come before Him with hearts wide open to worship Him in truth and in spirit, He will cause us to rise up with wings as eagles and to soar over the mountain tops. He will cause our enemies to bow down to us giving us victory in every situation regardless of the circumstances. God will allow us to move the mountains in our life just by simply speaking his Word and believing truth over a lie.

Let us draw near to our High Priest with a sincere heart in full assurance of faith to have our hearts cleansed from an evil conscience. Let us hold fast the confession of our hope without wavering, for Jesus is faithful. Let us consider how to stimulate and encourage one another to love and practice good deeds for the sake of the Kingdom of God.

Know that it is the presence of God within us that enables us to do all things. It is the presence of God's love that flows through us, one to another, if you have welcomed Jesus into your heart. If you haven't asked Him in, then you only possess human love. Human love is conditional because only God's love is unconditional. If you are weak, then understand that your strength comes from His love which conquers all things. It is only through Jesus our High Priest that we can love one another as we should.

CHAPTER TEN

Live Life Victoriously

*I*t is truly a humbling experience, to say the least, to see what your eternal future and everyone else's holds. It has definitely taught me to practice humility on a regular basis. I must search my heart with great courage to see where my morals and values stand, and I can't base my morals or values on my surroundings, but rather on the principles of the Most High God. I have learned not to compare myself with others, but instead just simply be open and honest with a willingness to be transparent before God. I must always remember to prepare myself daily for the moment when I meet my heavenly Father face to face.

Jesus has taught me that I must be honest with myself first before I can be honest with God, or anyone else for that matter. Being honest with my thoughts, feelings, actions and responses has brought me closer to the Lord. The more open I am about my own faults, the less I throw stones at someone else.

Judging others keeps us from receiving God's grace, for we will be judged in the same manner in which we judge others. I know that in my life I can't afford judgment because

I am guilty and need only mercy and grace to abound in my life, not judgment. We judge others and justify ourselves with our opinions. Well, our opinions won't heal us or cleanse us from unrighteousness! Therefore, it is essential that we lay our opinions down at the feet of Jesus, asking Him to transform our opinions into His thoughts of compassion, understanding and mercy for one another. We do all of this with the hope that we will escape eternal judgment.

> **Do not judge lest you be judged. For in the way you judge, you will be judged; and by your standard of measure, it will be measured to you. And why do you look at the speck that is in your brother's eye, but do not notice the log that is in your own eye? Or how can you say to your brother, Let me take the speck out of your eye, and behold, the log is in your own eye? You hypocrite, first take the log out of your own eye, and then you will see clearly to take the speck out of your brother's eye.**
> **Matthew 7:1-5 NASB**

How can we resolve our own issues if we continue to blame others for our own junk? Just because someone mistreats us doesn't give us the right to feel and act how we choose. It only gives us the opportunity to forgive and show grace. All of us have flaws and character defects, and each one of us must focus on working out our own salvation with fear and trembling. We must know we serve a mighty God who is the only true and just God. The Word teaches that to be the greatest is to become the least. We must let go of our attitudes of anger, resentment and self-righteousness.

Attitudes are simply feelings and opinions towards something, or they can be a mindset. Once we make the decision to deny the right to our own attitudes, our God is faithful enough to give us the tools to transform. We simply need to be obedient, knowing our heart will line up with our decisions.

I had to make a choice to change my inner thoughts. I had to stop entertaining thoughts of rejection such as, *They would be better off without me.*

When I would be in a room full of people I would begin to feel like a total outcast. I thought, *I'm different and I don't really fit in.* In my mind, others rejected me before they ever did in reality. I have made the choice to refuse to think those things. The minute I recognize the thoughts of rejection, I just say to myself, *No, I will not think that they will be better off without me because I have something that none of them have — me — and I am wonderfully made! I may be different, but isn't that what relationships are about - combining differences? If God thinks I am unique and precious in my own way, then I believe I am. God has adopted me into His family and therefore I walk in favor of all men by being accepted and appreciated.*

We are a spiritual being and the energy emanating from inside of our body is the state of our soul. Whether it's negative or positive, that energy will manifest itself. If you believe you are rejected, or that you're going to be rejected, then you will be rejected because what is on the inside of you reflects into your life. What comes from others can be dismissed and blocked from your soul.

Repentance seems to be a dirty word in the church world today. When people hear the word "repent" they claim you are being harsh, unaccepting and just too judgmental. Yet, repentance is truly the one thing that will allow God to come into your life and transform you. If we confess our sins, then God is faithful to forgive us and wash away our sins. Repentance is the act of our acknowledgment of our own sin and it is followed by a turning away from that sin.

If we have allowed rejection, bitterness, jealousy, anger or any other negative state to actually become a part of who we are, we need to repent. You can tell if a negative state is within you by recognizing how often you experience the emotion or thoughts.

If we confess our sins, He is faithful and righteous to forgive us our sins and to cleanse us from all unrighteousness.
1 John 1:9 NASB

When I realize I have fallen short, I am quick to repent because repentance doesn't happen only once in a person's life, it needs to happen every time we sin. I have learned that repentance brings restoration.

Therefore, if anyone is in Christ, he is a new creation; the old has gone, the new has come! All this is from God, who reconciled us to himself through Christ and gave us the ministry of reconciliation.
2 Corinthians 5:17-18 NIV

The Holy Spirit is so faithful to convict us of our sin and wrongdoings. Every one of us knows when we are wrong; it is a matter of being humble and honest enough to admit it to ourselves and then to God.

There are two forces at war with our soul: the force that is trying to keep us from freedom, and the force trying to set us free. The forces of evil can really only influence us in two different ways and that is through deception and temptation.

When deception or temptation leads us to continuously walk in disobedience to God, then we can develop strongholds in our mind which keep us bound. Strongholds can be passed down to us as children through the influence of others, or we can even develop them as adults. We will stay in bondage until we are willing to receive truth in these areas of our life. We must understand that a stronghold comes from being deceived by a lie told to us by the enemy.

Many times we remove ourselves from the protection of Christ by merely choosing to gratify our flesh. We believe the lie that we can't overcome our temptations because the desire is too strong, or that there is no harm in indulgence. Yet, the Word tells us that nothing is impossible through Christ who strengthens us.

Now the deeds of the flesh are evident, which are: immorality, impurity, sensuality, idolatry, sorcery, enmities, strife, jealousies, outbursts of anger, disputes, dissensions, factions, envy, drunkenness, carousing, and things like these; of which I forewarn you, just as I have forewarned you, that those who practice such things will not inherit the kingdom of God.
Galatians 5:19-21 NASB

No temptation has overtaken you except such as is common to man; and God is faithful, who will not allow you to be tempted beyond what you are able, but with the temptation will provide the way of escape also, that you may be able to endure it.
1 Corinthians 10:13 NASB

As I have matured in my walk with Christ, I have learned that every time I get tempted to go astray, I must double-check my heart to see if I am really trusting God completely. I have realized that when I want only temporary pleasures, then my focus is on me and I fall short every time. Yet, when I look past the immediate comfort and look at the greater picture, I am allowing the Holy Spirit to keep my focus on Him and victory always follows.

Salvation is freely given to all, yet disobedience keeps us from receiving the entirety of our blessings. When we walk in disobedience, we make ourselves susceptible to evil. You must know that the Lord is by your side and is willing and able to set you free from all of your afflictions.

Many are the afflictions of the righteous, but the LORD delivereth him out of them all.
Psalm 34:19 KJV

We have been entrusted with God's authority and power to claim over our lives. This is available because Christ, our God, has chosen to dwell within us to make us His Holy Temple. We can go boldly into His Holy Place to find grace and ask for what it is we desire, and if we ask anything according to the will of the Father, then it shall be granted to us. It is God's will that all be restored, renewed and set free from evil in every form. It is simply a choice and decision that each one must make: do we want freedom or bondage?

Rest assured that He who began a good work in you will complete it until the day of Christ, the day when our God shall return in the clouds of glory to claim His bride. That will be a day of great rejoicing, for all sorrow shall come to an end and all the things we have hoped for will come to pass. No temptation in this life is worth costing you your soul.

Take into consideration that every little decision you make has the potential to make a major impact on your life. The accumulation of little decisions creates the big picture of your decisive will.

May your will be turned over to the renewing power of the Holy Spirit to wash you and cleanse you while transforming you into perfect love. May we receive the fullness of God's blessings according to His perfect will which He has already determined for each one of us. Let not a single one of us fall short from God's perfect will for our life. May the Light rule and reign within us every moment of every day.

CHAPTER ELEVEN

A Servant's Heart

The journey of my life thus far has been an incredible adventure. I have gone from an emotionally distraught, lonely, depressed and hopeless individual to one who has purpose and an abundance of love deep within me. An important lesson I have learned is that if your soul does not possess a Godly character trait, then you cannot give it or share it with someone else. If I have no peace in my soul, thoughts or emotions, then I can't give peace to others through my words or attitudes. If the atmosphere around me is full of strife, then I must look inward and recognize that strife is probably a part of who I am and it must be separated from my thoughts and actions.

We are sojourners on this earth and we will not be here forever. We are simply like pilgrims in a foreign hemisphere. We are on a tremendous journey and every choice we make creates a little alteration in our soul. Our thoughts and actions make transformations in our minds, perspectives, and on our emotional states and end up directing our will towards the destiny of our choice.

Delivered

Many people are confused and complacent about spiritual matters. Some who believe there is a God mistakenly believe that every "good" person goes to heaven. Another erroneous belief is that there is no spiritual existence at all. To these people, death is a mystery and when the physical body ceases to work, there is nothingness. Others like to believe that if they do exist after death, they can deal with it, and if there is nothing left, they will never know. They approach eternal life just as they deal with everyday living by solving the problems as they come up.

This complete ignorance will permanently destroy people. We are spiritual beings who will live forever. The word forever doesn't have the power or the revelation we need because everything in this life has an end. We can't humanly grasp "no ending".

I feel so inadequate when trying to explain these spiritual concepts, and I often get frustrated and even angry because I cannot adequately communicate spirit to flesh or physical to eternal. The Holy Spirit is the only one who can give you the spiritual revelation and wisdom to understand the things of God

Our soul is like a piece of clay or a material which is moldable or pliable. The words we speak, the music we listen to and all the things we watch, see or read take a part in shaping our soul. All the things that come through our five senses are molding our soul into a permanent form. Sight, hearing, taste, touch and smell are the senses which lead to the gateways into your soul.

In life you have the choice to become either a follower of "light"(Jesus) or "darkness." (our enemy) Our souls existed years before technology provided the luxury of so many options of transportation. Today you can travel quickly over water, land and air, but it wasn't that long ago when you had two choices of travel: you could either walk or ride an animal. That was it!

It is the same concept we have been given with our soul. Either we choose to transform it into God's image and love, or we allow it to be full of fear which is from the pits of Hell. Ideally oil and water should not come out of the same well just as the character of God and the character of the enemy should not come out of the same person. We cannot serve two masters because you will become like one or the other, but never should we allow the merging of the two.

This is the core of spiritual warfare which is the battle being waged within you between good and evil. We were created in the image of God. We were designed to be the sons of God for the purpose of exalting our King and living in His love. We are to be eager to return to a pure, unified state of existence through the spiritual transference of open communication with Him.

To be a servant of Christ is to return the love which He gave to us back again to Him in worship and praise. However, if we do not allow love to become a part of us, then we are not capable of servant hood.

Love is not just caring, it is a state of being shaped by the character traits of God which reside in us as true believers. Love is kind, patient and envies no one. Love is never boastful, conceited, rude or selfish and is not quick to take offense.

Love keeps no score of wrongs nor does it gloat over another's sins, but it always delights in truth. There is nothing love cannot face and there is no limit to its faith, hope and its endurance.

A servant gives generous, loving service to his or her Master and is eager to perform the desires of their King. Servants are not bitter, nor do they serve with ulterior motives. Rather, their hearts are pure and they desire only to please the One who has called and continues to sustain them.

Many times in my life I have been kind to others by lending a helping hand, offering my time in their hour of need and giving things that I thought others needed. The reality is that all these acts of goodness were simply done in vain because my true heart's motive was only to be a good person and not to act for the sake of righteousness on behalf of my Master. Being a good person only breeds temporary satisfaction, but doing good deeds for the sake of Jesus and His righteousness brings eternal rewards.

Instead of striving every day for my own agenda, I encourage myself to seek for the Holy Spirit to search my heart to reveal to me his will and purpose for the day. I ask to be used as a vessel to accomplish His will. I pray that my heart and soul will continually be changed into that of a trustworthy servant, a servant who is faithful and loyal at all times.

God pours His spirit into our body like we pour water into a glass. The problem we face is that God is not being seen in His people because we are a body full of compromise and sin and we're lacking in spiritual understanding.

I encourage you to believe by faith that God's presence, a part of His being, is actually being placed into your body. Recognize that we are the Temple of God with His Holy Spirit residing within us. Believe we can ask His Holy Spirit to clothe our soul with the cleansing of the blood of Christ and ask that the washing of God's word bathe our mind with His waterfall of truth. With our permission and co-operation He can transform us into a purified vessel, a vessel cleansed from all unrighteousness and worthy of an intimate relationship with God himself. We are either a vessel of honor or one of dishonor.

A vessel of honor will live a life of forgiving others and unconditionally loving those who you come into contact with. This vessel makes a decision not to allow any form of prejudice to sway its thoughts and actions and treats all people as equals despite race, status or education. A vessel of dishonor is a soul who chooses to entertain thoughts of rebellion or disinterest toward God and one who seeks self satisfaction.

Fear shapes a soul which only thinks of self. This one is full of revenge, rejection, violence, murder, loneliness and guilt. Other ungodly traits include lying, jealousy, perversion, lust, bitterness, revenge, vindictive behavior, unforgiveness and every unpleasant trait we can imagine.

So many people are operating in fear and intimidation and are always seeking a means to survive. They're left with an emotional void and mental confusion which only continues to escalate. Their desperate cries get louder and louder when no answer is in sight. This is because they are serving the wrong master.

If we allowed our surroundings or experiences to mold us, then we would be a people filled with isolation and hurt and would be incapable of serving God. All of us go through tragic experiences which result in painful repercussions to one degree or another. We all have the choice to either allow God to exchange beauty for our ashes or to go hopeless.

I lived in loneliness and I chose to escape through an intimate relationship with Christ. I wallowed in self-pity, feeling sorry for myself and making excuses for my wretchedness. I lived in blame for many years and always pointed my finger at everyone else for what they did to me. Now I receive the responsibility for my own feelings. I accept the fact that internal and eternal freedom is a choice which is made every moment of every day. I have chosen to be free to love and not hate and to be free to do what is right in the eyes of God and not in the eyes of others. I chose to be free to live and not die.

Each step I take I am learning new lessons that teach me how to become a more effective servant: lessons that correct me when I am wrong, instruct me down the right path, encourage me to do better and lessons that remind me that the important things are seen in the simplicities of our lives.

The Holy Spirit has used the relationships in my life to equip me for the tasks I have to overcome. These relationships also give me the companionship I desire. I believe our relationships dictate whether we go down the narrow road that leads to eternal victory or the broad path that leads to destruction. Our friends do influence the choices we make, and they can sway us to the left or the right. I have made a conscious effort to guard myself and my family from relationships which have a negative impact upon our thinking, and I have chosen to surround us with people who encourage us in our faith and service to Christ.

Every little decision we make has the potential of having a major impact on our eternal future! This is why it is so important to be as wise as a serpent and as harmless as a dove, seeking truth in all that we do. Our lives only have real meaning if we live for our eternal purpose and not the monetary and temporal pleasures of this life. I want every decision I make to reflect the dedication and steadfastness I have to my Lord and Savior. I want to live my life searching for truth, for it is the truth that shall set us free to know God and walk according to His purposes.

If we seek, then we shall find; if we knock, the doors will be opened to us; if we diligently seek wisdom, we shall receive it, for not one good thing will be withheld from a child of God. Our future is filled with promise and hope. We can be rest assured knowing that if we surrender to God and give Him the control He desires to have in our lives, all the promises of prosperity will come to pass in our lives. They will also be passed down to the lives of our children as well as our children's children. The great I Am is a giving God who desires only the best for us, but unfortunately only a few receive the best because only dedicated obedience on our part allows the blessings to flow through us and around us.

Our heavenly Father desires to dwell in us and move through us. He has made us to be vessels of honor and not dishonor, extensions of His hands to reach out to the brokenhearted, a voice to proclaim victory in the middle of the storms of life, to be His arms that embrace those who have been abandoned and to be His feet to go wherever He calls us to go.

We live in a world full of evil, but the evil doesn't have to penetrate us or take away our eternal hope. No matter what you have gone through in your past or what you are currently experiencing, it will never separate you from the love of Christ Jesus. Don't ever mistake some vain acts of religion for the love of God because once you've been touched by the Master and you will never be the same.

My heart's desire is that you will see truth clearly and that you will run towards it with all that is in you. You will not stop until you have embraced the One who has the authority to save. It is our responsibility to lay down our rebellion and totally surrender to the authority God has over our lives. We should be serving Him with our whole heart. He is the perfect gentleman and gives us a choice to love Him back and become His servant. He will never force you. He simply is asking you to bow at His feet in love and obedience and to receive wholeness and fullness of life as He intended. We can either choose to have our rewards now and face the consequences for eternity, or we can choose to press towards a higher calling and reap eternal life. It is your choice to make and I pray that you make the choice of a wise person, not a foolish one.

Being a slave to sin is a slow transformation of forming your soul into a person of sorrow and pain who always suffers from a victim mentality. Believing the lie that you are not in control of your own life, and allowing others to dictate how you feel and what happens to you is not what He intended. If you are powerless over your own soul and are continuing to do the very things you despise, worship will break the chains of bondage.

I have learned that God not only wants praise and worship from His servants, but He also instructs us to shout with a voice of victory proclaiming things that aren't as though they already are. We can actually call His will into existence through our faith. He is a God who asks us to surrender our spirit of heaviness in exchange for the garments of praise, and He desires to give us joy for our mourning. He will take all the ashes from our life and turn them into beauty. He'll take all the tragedies that happen to us and exchange them for victories. I serve a God who brings healing to the sick, one who restores the soul and binds up the wounds of the brokenhearted. He is a God of love and only pours goodness upon His people.

It is truly the love of God that has brought restoration, healing and every good thing into my life. I have been changed from a slave into a servant. I am so grateful to share the goodness of my Lord and tell all who are willing to hear how I have been eternally delivered.

Prayer of Salvation

*T*o make Jesus the Lord of your life, you need to make this confession:
Jesus, I confess with my mouth and believe in my heart that You are Lord. I believe that You died on the cross and were raised from the dead. By the power of the blood You shed, I ask that You cleanse me from all unrighteousness and deliver me from all my bondage. Devil and demon forces — get out of my life — for you no longer have authority over me because Jesus is now my Lord and Savior. Jesus, I thank You for Your saving grace and I ask that You write my name down in the Lamb's Book of Life. Thank You for giving me a sincere heart that I may believe in You, and I thank You that I will spend eternity with You. I will be forever grateful that Your Spirit has drawn me to Your feet, and I am now your servant. Use me to glorify Your name.
Amen.

Closing Prayer

Oh my Father, thank You for Your unprecedented, unfailing love. Thank You for the free gift of salvation and for paying the price for my soul. I will never understand the cost associated with the debt You paid for me on the cross. Thank you for the blood of Jesus that was shed for each and every one of us so that each may have the opportunity to know You. May Your praises rule and reign in my heart forever, making melody to my Savior and Deliverer. Place a dance upon my feet and a song in my heart that I may sing and dance before Your throne, praising You with my whole heart, holding nothing back, standing before You transparent of and all allowing You to transform me into a being who is pleasing to you. Take all our afflictions, sorrows and confusion and turn them into something beautiful. May our lives become a sweet aroma drifting up to your throne. Thank You for Your saving grace and mercy that endures forever. Receive us as we are and mold us; make us as we ought to be. We surrender all to you and your throne. Praise be unto the most High God. Glory and Honor to the Highest. Your perfect will be done in each and every life.
  Amen

CPSIA information can be obtained at www.ICGtesting.com
Printed in the USA
LVOW041424120812

293983LV00004B/39/P